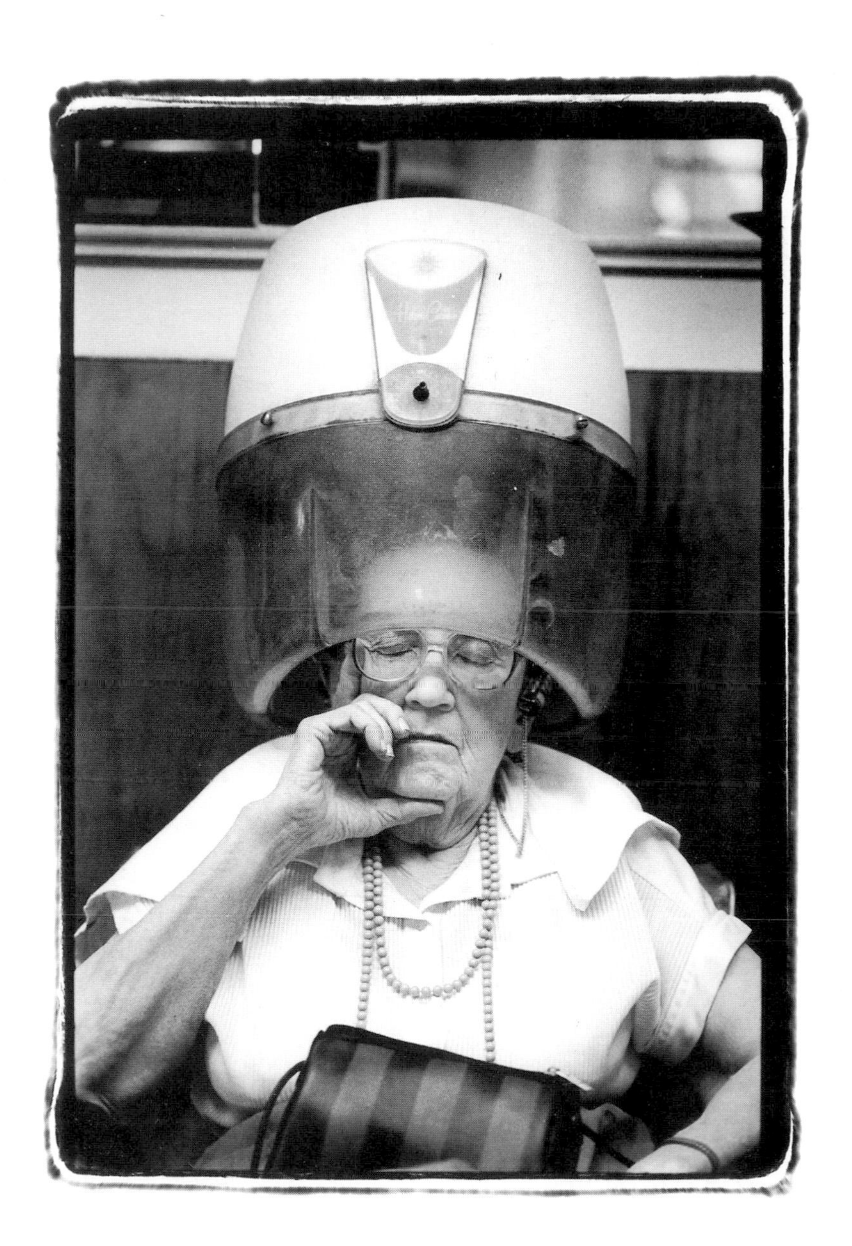

Beauty Box

A tribute to the legendary beauty parlors of the South

■

TEXT BY KATHY KEMP

PHOTOGRAPHS BY KARIM SHAMSI-BASHA

CRANE HILL
PUBLISHERS

Published by Crane Hill Publishers, 3608 Clairmont Avenue, Birmingham, AL 35222;
www.cranehill.com

Printed in China

Library of Congress Cataloging-in-Publication Data

Kemp, Kathy, 1954-
The beauty box: a tribute to the legendary beauty parlors of the South/text by Kathy Kemp;
photographs by Karim Shamsi-Basha.
p. cm.
ISBN 1-881548-88-0
1. Beauty shops—Southern States. 2. Beauty shops—Southern States—Pictorial works.
I. Shamsi-Basha, Karim, 1965- II. Title.
TT958.K46 1997
646.7'2'0975—dc21 97-22803
CIP

10 9 8 7 6 5 4 3 2 1

For Helen Mary "Pud" Crider Sharp Strickland,
also known as "Tootie"; for George Strickland;
and in memory of John Crider.
—Kathy Kemp

For my wife, Dee, my jewel, whose support and encouragement
made it possible for me to do the traveling necessary to
complete this book. She has dedicated her life to others in a
way that no one can match.
And for my sons Zade and Dury, the cutest boys on earth.
—Karim Shamsi-Basha

To Susan,
Best wishes.
Kathy Kemp
12/7/98

To Susan:
have many happy
hair days!
Karim

Table of Contents

Acknowledgments

Special thanks and love to Kathy's mom, Dru Kemp; her aunt, Virginia Cowden; her brother and sister-in-law, John and Donna Kemp; her nieces Hollie, Lauren, and Katie Kemp; her nephew Brandon Kemp; Karim's mom and dad, Laila and Kheridean Shamsi-Basha; his "other parents," Wayne and Erna Tipps; and his sister-in-law, Shelley Keeley. Their love and support through the years have meant so much.

Special thanks to Kay Argo; to Jeff Brown for his copyediting skills; to friends at the *Birmingham Post-Herald* and *The Birmingham News;* and to the staff at Crane Hill Publishers, including Ellen Sullivan, Bob Weathers, Scott Fuller, Catherine O'Hare, Lee Howard, Amy Robertson Boyd, and Leeth Grissom. Extra special thanks to our Crane Hill editor, Norma McKittrick, whose enthusiasm, patience, and talent helped make this book possible.

Thanks to all the wonderful beauty parlor operators and their friendly and entertaining customers for their acceptance and friendship.

And most of all thanks to God, for keeping safe watch over Karim and allowing us one more chance to work together.

Introduction

When I was six years old, my mother decided I should become beautiful. So she loaded me into our 1953 Chevy BelAir and headed to Powderly, then a fairly rural community on the southwest side of Birmingham, Alabama, where I grew up.

My mother's beautician was known simply as Miz Mack. Her shop was in the basement of her home. I don't know if Mack was her first name or last, but I do recall that she had a husband, as well as a pug dog with eyes that popped, unpredictably and inexplicably, clean out of his head.

I didn't wish to get beautified, but then I don't recall the subject being up for discussion. Mother parked the BelAir outside Miz Mack's shingled house, near the tree with the tire swing dangling from a limb. Miz Mack's husband's semi rig sat in the shade of that big oak tree. We walked past it toward the basement door, which opened into a pink-and-white universe filled with sinks, dryers, and enough secondhand hair spray to merit a warning from the U.S. Surgeon General.

I sat in a green padded-vinyl swivel chair in front of a long mirror and watched Miz Mack, in her white nurse's uniform, chop off several inches of my long tangled hair. And that was just for starters. Once she finished chopping, the beautician commenced to give me what the ladies called a permanent wave, using tiny rubber rollers and potions that made my eyes water.

When we finally got back in the BelAir for the drive home, I looked like a pint-size Ethel Mertz. Tight chestnut-colored curls clung to the back of my scarlet neck. A few weeks later, when the Robert E. Lee Elementary School photographer snapped my first-grade portrait, I was still scowling.

That turned out to be my first bad-hair day. I still wonder sometimes what my mother was thinking, especially since I'd heard her say, repeatedly, that Miz Mack had butchered my adorable cousin Karen, whose raven natural curls were never quite as lovely once the beautician gave them a whack.

In any event, I've come to realize that going to the beauty parlor isn't solely, or even necessarily, about becoming beautiful.

For my mother and other women of a certain generation, it had more to do with friendship, ritual, gossip, and simply needing a reason to get out of the house. Back then only the severely disturbed paid for psychotherapy. Ordinary women worked out their troubles during their weekly visits to the beauty shop.

Nancy Frascatore holding a newspaper article about her brother Albert, who made her beauty shop ladies "feel like queens for a day."

It's those women and their beauticians that we celebrate with this book. Photographer Karim Shamsi-Basha and I traveled many miles over many months in search of old-fashioned beauty parlors with old-fashioned clientele. Although such shops exist all over the United States, we decided to focus on the Deep South, including Florida and Texas, because, generally speaking, no other region produces so much big hair—or so many tall tales.

In many ways the old-fashioned Southern beauty shop is a folk tradition that seems fast on its way to extinction. Younger, working women can't imagine sitting under a hair dryer every week when a bimonthly cut-and-style and a daily home shampoo require less time, energy, and probably money.

What turns up missing from that progressive routine are the characters and drama that inspire uniquely Southern works of art. A few years back Louisiana playwright Robert Harling lovingly immortalized the old-timey Southern beauty parlor with his wonderful ensemble stage comedy *Steel Magnolias.* Harling's beautician was a big-bosomed gal with an even bigger heart. Her customers included a youngish socialite, a lovable curmudgeon, and the widow of the town's former mayor.

The characters shared joys, heartaches, gossip, and belly laughs—all at the same time, every week, in this small-town carport house-of-beauty. Harling's play proved such a success that Hollywood turned it into a movie, starring big-bosomed, big-hearted, and big-haired Dolly Parton as the beautician, with an all-star supporting cast. On paper it sounded like a hit. But on the movie screen Harling's story fell flatter than a year-old perm.

The problem? After much pondering, I think I've figured it out. Hollywood took much of the action, which Harling had set entirely in the beauty shop, and spread it all over the fictional town. Suddenly the unique reason for such diverse characters to come together was no longer there.

That more or less illustrates the point of this book—that the beauty parlor itself just may be the star.

My mother, by the way, has changed beauticians several times in the years since my inaugural visit to Miz Mack. Her reasons were never flighty. One of her old beauticians moved. Others retired. At least one died. She's been with her current beauty operator, Nancy Frascatore, for a dozen years. They meet every Friday at 11 a.m. at Nancy's storefront salon in Birmingham.

Although Nancy is a fine hair-doer, for many years she offered an extra bonus to the ladies who visited her shop. Nancy's younger brother, Albert Zegarelli, would greet the customers with a kiss, a bow, and a dance. Although Albert was in his fifties then, Down's syndrome had rendered him an eternal child. More than one doctor suggested Nancy put him in an institution. Instead, she took him everywhere she went, including her salon, where he made the ladies feel like queens for a day. Albert also made them count their blessings.

It's been several years now since Albert died of complications from diabetes. But his picture is on the wall, and the dance music still plays on the radio. My mother hasn't stopped telling Nancy how to do hair, and Nancy still doesn't listen.

If her customers get too bossy, Nancy reminds them that years ago she went to beauty college with a young operator named Wynette Byrd, who later became known to the world as country music superstar Tammy Wynette. That gets them to oohing and aahing.

Nancy also tells off-color jokes, and her customers feign shock and hold their ears, careful not to crush their new hairdos. They read *Ladies Home Journal* and *The National Enquirer,* gossip, giggle, drink Cokes out of the bottle, sample each other's pound cake, mourn each other's dead husbands, and talk about everything under the sun. Nobody's in much of a hurry to leave, unless rain is in the forecast. Then the rush is on to protect their coiffures, which couldn't be moved by a hurricane. Their hairdos are as strong and true as the ladies themselves.

And that's the beauty of it.

Kathy Kemp

Birmingham, Alabama
August 1998

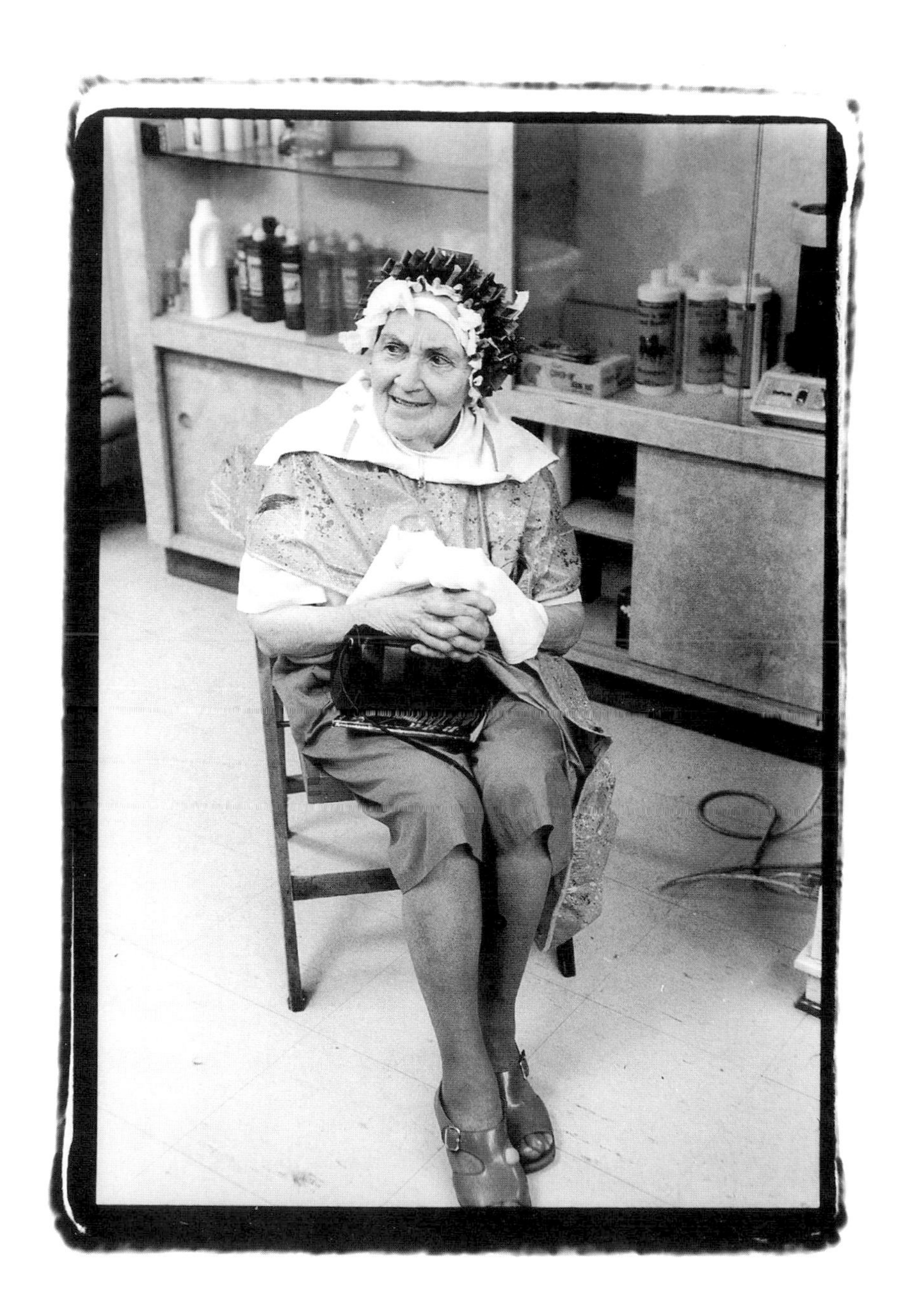

The Beauty Box

■

BIRMINGHAM
ALABAMA

In the back room of a tan clapboard house east of downtown, Farie Ray Liner sits under a hair dryer, smoking a Salem and sipping a bottled Coke, which altogether is quite a feat considering that she's also undergoing the beauty-parlor equivalent of brain surgery—a French manicure.

"Be still, Farie," commands sixty-nine-year-old Nettie Hyatt, a sweet-faced grandmother who seems incapable of raising her voice. Not that Mrs. Liner could hear if she did—that hair dryer roars louder than the window air conditioner.

"Normally I charge seven dollars, but the French job is ten," Nettie confides as she paints white half-moon tips on Mrs. Liner's pink nails. So experienced a manicurist is Nettie that she doesn't have to use the nail guides that come in the French manicure box.

"I had a doctor tell me I'd have made a good surgeon, my hands are so steady," she says. "If you watch what I'm doing, you'll see that the whole time, I'm massaging the nail. That gets the blood flowing. It stimulates the nail and the cuticle too. I did a nurse once, and she said, 'Nettie, that should be a treatment instead of a manicure.' "

"People need a place to vent their anxieties. So we tune in or out, whichever works better at the time."

In her all-white ensemble of slacks, blouse, and comfortable shoes, Nettie wouldn't look out of place in the emergency room. Of course when she's conducting an operation like Mrs. Liner's French manicure, she dons additional protective gear—a flowery pink-and-blue smock that complements her eyes and skin.

Mrs. Liner, on the other hand, is dressed in red, white, and blue in honor of the July Fourth holiday. Her fingers are adorned with more stones than a bad gallbladder. Through the years Mrs. Liner's family did well in Birmingham in the restaurant and nightclub business. But these days the sixty-year-old widow knows those good ol' times are far behind.

"I've got a thirty-five-year-old daughter with terminal cancer," Mrs. Liner says. "She's the only child I'll ever have. Will you say a prayer for her?"

The entire clientele of the Beauty Box is praying for Mrs. Liner's daughter. That's because the little tan clapboard house is more than just a beauty shop. Besides maintaining standing weekly appointments that sometimes don't change for decades, the Beauty Box ladies cultivate friendships almost as important to them as church, children, and long-dead husbands. And their beauticians are the only therapists most will ever have.

"We're sounding boards, I guess you'd say," explains Lola Webb, who has owned the Beauty Box since 1958 and has fixed hair for three generations. "People need a place to vent their anxieties. So we tune in or out, whichever works better at the time."

While Nettie works on Mrs. Liner in the back room, Lola—along with Gail Smith, the shop's only other beautician—does hair in the front room. There, a half-dozen conversations go on at once, while in

the adjacent kitchen Oprah holds court on a small black-and-white TV with aluminum foil wrapped around the antenna.

Both Lola and Gail are too down-to-earth to call themselves "stylists." The difference between a stylist and a beautician, Lola says, is that a stylist has her nose in the air.

"They're the same damn thing," she says. "The only thing stylists do that we don't is run you all over creation while your head's wet. You get washed over here, cut over there, and combed out and sprayed down across the room. That way they can charge you more. We do it all while you're sitting in one place."

At the Beauty Box, a shampoo-and-set runs you $8, and a haircut is $8 more.

"Well I went off, and when I got back, she was green. I didn't tell her. Nooooo sirree."

A permanent, which most of the ladies get three times a year, costs $35 and up. Color, which they get more often but won't admit, is $20, though it's $35 if you're talking bleach.

A good-natured blond who, at age sixty-five, looks remarkably like the mature Rosemary Clooney, Lola prides herself on her skill with color. Not that there hasn't been a mishap or two. "See, the customers do a little fibbing to you occasionally," Lola says. "I asked this girl what she'd been putting on her hair. She said, 'Nothin'.' Well, you shouldn't lie to your beautician.

"Her hair looked red, so I told her I'd stay with that same color. She said, 'That's fine 'cause I'm a natural redhead.'

Well I went off, and when I got back, she was green. I didn't tell her. Noooooo sirree. I said, 'You lie there. I've got to go mix up something else.' She went out a redhead, but I'm telling you, it took some doin'."

In the four decades that Lola's been a beautician, the single thing that's changed most in the hair-doin' business is color, she says. "The government came in and screwed it all up. The cancer thing, you know. I used to do more color than anybody on the east side of town. I could do all the formulas, make it come out just like I wanted it. When the government got through, nothin' worked. I almost gave up on it. Now if I see something that says 'new and improved,' I run like crazy."

"We did that beehive, Honey," Lola says. "Lord, you'd tease and lacquer, tease and lacquer, 'til it looked like 'The Simpsons.'"

Hairstyles, of course, have also changed. No sooner had beauticians mastered the Talullah Bankhead flip and the Doris Day pixie than along came the 1960s and a hairdo that resembled the Leaning Tower of Pisa.

"We did that beehive, Honey," Lola says. "Lord, you'd tease and lacquer, tease and lacquer, 'til it looked like *The Simpsons.*

"I had this one lady, cute as a button, she came in and said, 'Red and I are going out tonight, so do me something

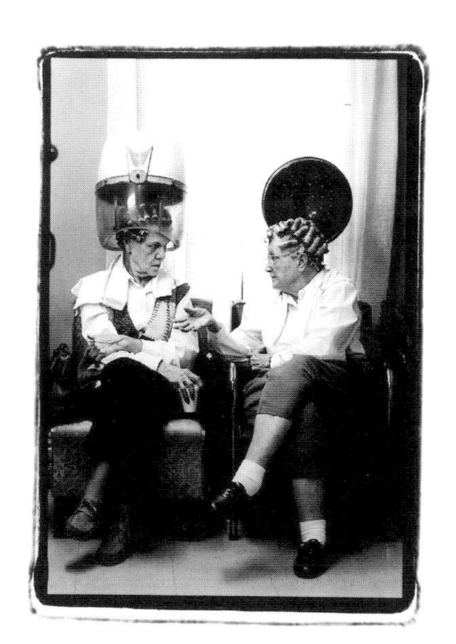

real fancy.' I said, 'Well what, Margaret?' She said, 'Big, you know.' So I did, and I sent her home, and Honey, in thirty minutes, she was back. I said, 'What's wrong?' She said, 'He won't go with me like this.'

"I said, 'Margaret, you don't have time for me to do it over.' Because when you put that darn lacquer on there, I want to tell you, it's staying up for a week. I said, 'Come in here, and we'll mash it.' And that's what we did. We mashed it and mashed it, and he took her out."

While Lola takes a barbecue sandwich break in the kitchen, Gail—who's done hair at the Beauty Box for thirty-one years—is telling a story about barbecue for the fourth time in less than two hours. That's because every time a new lady sits down in the brown vinyl chair at Gail's station, Gail is asked what she did for the Fourth of July.

"We bought barbecue the night before and it smelled so good, we had to eat some right then," Gail tells a customer wearing purple pants, who's just settled down for a hair washing. "We bought too much, but I'd sooner have to throw it out the door than not have enough."

Verta Hicks, the lady in purple, asks Gail about her recent trip to Florida. "Bet you had a good time," Mrs. Hicks says.

Gail, recapping another story for the umpteenth time, says, "Yeah, but the beach was messed up bad. The ocean was terrible. It smelled awful. You couldn't walk outside without getting respiratory problems, headaches, and diarrhea."

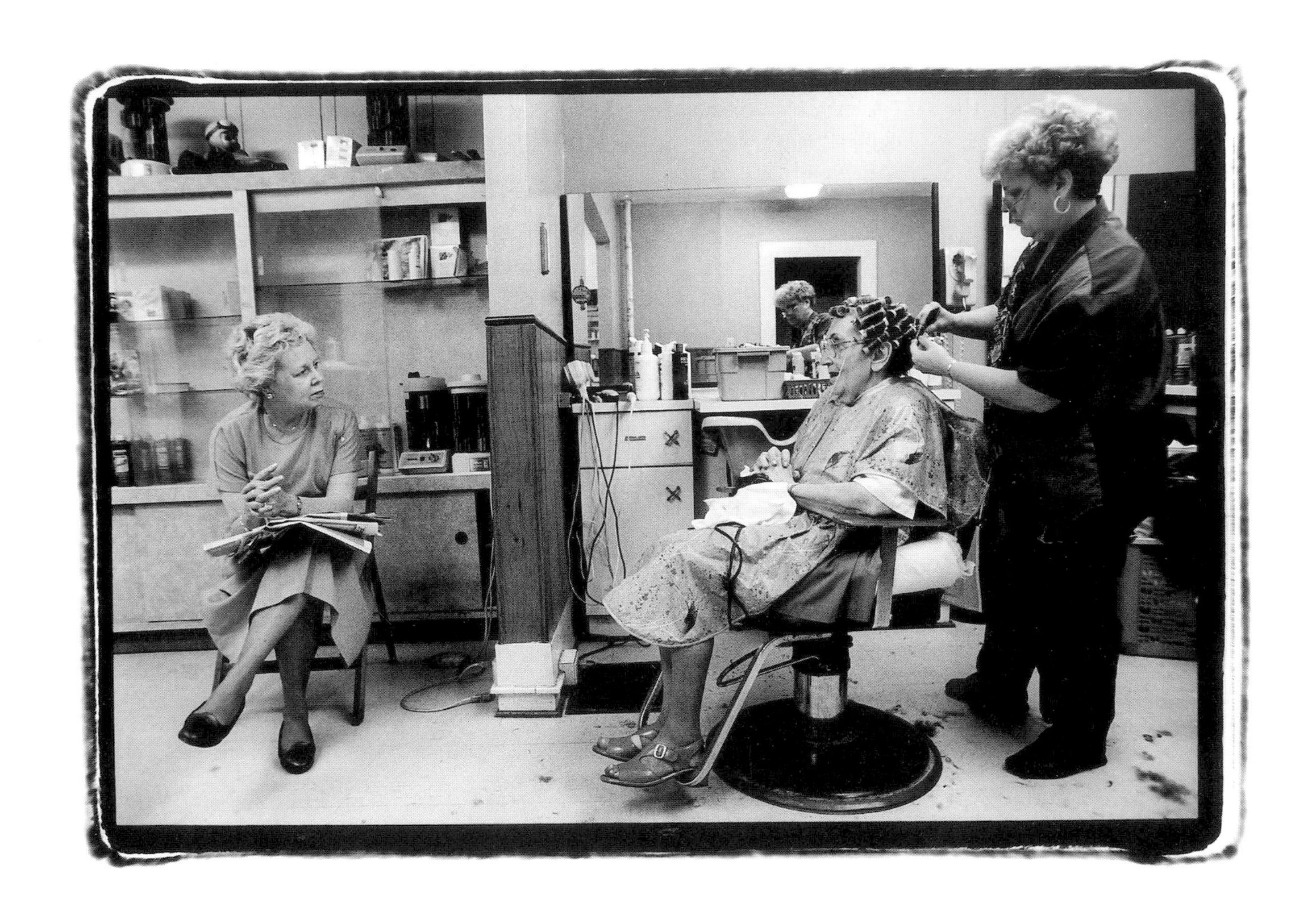

"Sunburn's bad enough, without all that," Mrs. Hicks observes and then switches gears. "Mildred let that youngest grandson of hers drive that big yellow car. I can't imagine it. She must really love that boy."

Mrs. Hicks, who's had a standing appointment at 2:30 every Friday afternoon for a dozen years, waves at Pauline Felder, a friend from church who's under the dryer. A widow until six years ago, when she met a retired navy man in a senior citizens' singing group, Mrs. Hicks can't say enough about Gail's skill with hair.

"She just goes out of her way to make it perfect," Mrs. Felder agrees, prompting Gail to stop what she's doing and respond. "Let's don't get too sickening, Pauline."

In the meantime Agnes de Shazo—who read the entire *National Enquirer* while sitting under the hair dryer—is at Lola's station waiting to have her new permanent uncoiled. Cute and spry, in snazzy blue-striped pants and matching sweater, Mrs. de Shazo loves to talk, except when she's asked her age, which draws a long silence and finally this response: "I'm retired thirty-six years."

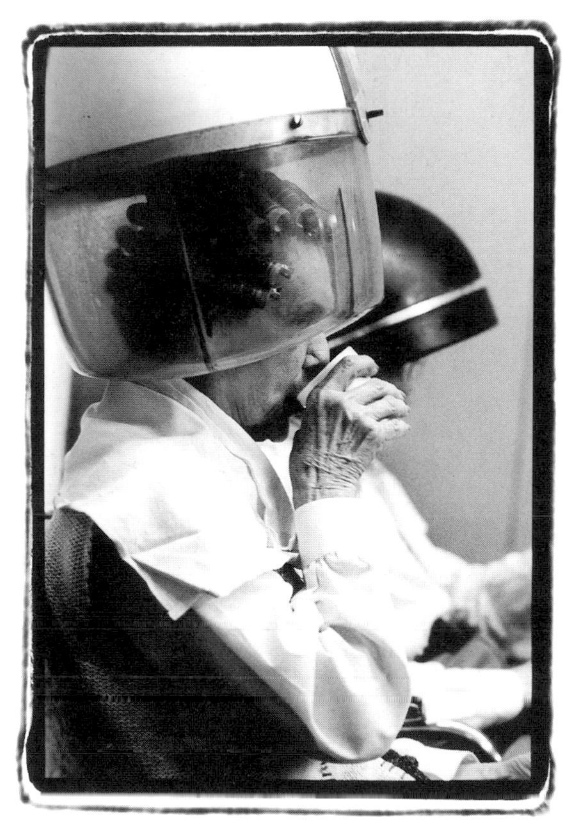

Then she's off and running. "It's de Shazo, with a little 'd.' It's French, you know. Bear Bryant's my second cousin. My son's a doctor, and my granddaughter just graduated summa cum laude." She further states, with no prompting, that she's a retired dental hygienist who now volunteers with the humane society and the chamber of commerce.

Lola, who's done Mrs. de Shazo's hair for going on forty years, hears it all, yet utters not a word. But she can't conceal that hint of amusement in her eyes. Mrs. de Shazo continues, "Somebody hit the side of my Cadillac over there in front of Bruno's, and I just got it back today."

"You've got to love the people."

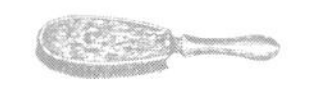

Two more ladies come through the glass-paned double front doors, and soon the multiple conversations seem to mesh into a single discombobulated narrative.

Lola: "I was sound asleep at nine o'clock."

Mrs. de Shazo: "I like to read before I go to sleep. I've got so many books. I even bought that one about that woman who drowned her two kids."

Mrs. Felder, rustling papers: "I just had to have three cancers removed from my face. I brought my insurance down to study it."

Mrs. Liner to Nettie: "They can't much tell the difference between indigestion and heartburn. That's what they told my brother."

Somebody asks Lola where her twenty-four-year-old daughter, Wendy, lives. "Near the Clothes Horse," Lola says.

"Do they have cute clothes?" another lady asks.

Mrs. de Shazo gets up and goes to a mirror to paint her lips the same shade of red as her long fingernails. Gussie Mills, who's out from under the dryer, declares, "I feel real cute," after Mrs. de Shazo tells her she looks pretty.

Mrs. Mills isn't one of the Friday regulars. Normally her appointment is Thursday morning at 9:30, but she had to come today because of the holiday. A retired grade-school teacher, Mrs. Mills looks forward to her weekly visit. "Everything here is so pleasant," she says. "For a busy housewife, this is the kind of shop you need."

"In my estimation, you go not only to get yourself fixed but also to socialize."

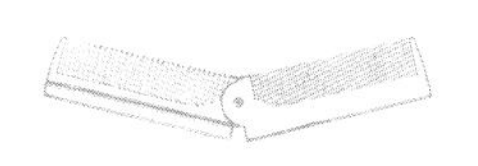

Not only do the beauticians "understand my hair," she says, "but if it came down to it, they know things about me that close friends would know. They hear the problems of the world. I lost my husband not long back, and I don't know what I would have done without this hour every week."

Mrs. Mills, like most of the Beauty Box ladies, is well beyond retirement age, yet, thanks to her beautician, it's hard to tell. "Just say I'm in my seventies. That's lying. I'm older than people think I look."

Gail, who's trimming one of the newcomers, repeats the barbecue story. Then her gray-haired fiftyish client recounts her trials and tribulations at work. "I got my job evaluation, and she put down I was hard to work with. Can you believe that? Terry says she's jealous because I get along with all the men."

Mrs. de Shazo, meanwhile, gets friskier and friskier. "I got to go see Dr. McCullough and get me a face-lift," she tells Lola. "I might want to get me a boyfriend."

"You've got to love the people," Gail says, explaining what drew her to the beauty business. "Most operators move along a lot, but I never wanted to. I love the clientele here. I love the freedom I have to discuss my beliefs and how I feel about things. A lot of the talk is church related. We get hot and heavy over politics sometimes."

In the heyday of the Beauty Box, Gail was one of five operators doing some 250 hairdos a week. For years, though, it's been just her and Lola serving a little over a hundred ladies Tuesdays through Saturdays.

Gail, who grew up in the community of Adamsville on the west side of Birmingham, isn't from the big city. Neither is Lola—she was born in rural Walker County, Alabama, where her father was a coal contractor until the Great Depression drove him out of work. Then he became a machinist who also had a knack for real estate.

"Dad would buy a house, and if someone came along and offered him a thousand more than he paid for it, we were gone," Lola says. "During the war, I can remember, we got to where we didn't even unpack. I think we moved every month one year. I don't see how I ever passed in school."

"We get hot and heavy over politics sometimes."

But she did, and after graduating from high school, Lola briefly went to Jacksonville State University, figuring on becoming a teacher. She quickly decided that wasn't for her. So she moved to Birmingham and went to work as a secretary in a one-girl office.

By then married to Charles Webb, Lola worked for the same man for eight years before the job changed and she decided to leave. Scanning the newspaper want ads day after day, she kept seeing the same advertisement for a secretary at a local steel company. "I saw the ad so often, I thought, 'This is an old codger who's hard to get along with.' I decided to apply 'cause it was so close to home.

"So I did, and I was not there ten minutes 'til he told me all his secretaries slept with him. I thought, 'So that's why this ad's been in there so long.' He just said it out of the blue. I said, 'I want to tell you what. I believe I've come to the wrong place. Number one, I don't participate in such. And number two, you aren't my damn type.'" She cackles at the recollection.

Fed up with the idea of working for men, Lola decided to go into the beauty business. In 1957 she enrolled in the old Cargyle Beauty College in downtown Birmingham. The next year, when she got her beautician's license, she bought an eastside shop called the Beauty Box, then in a brick office building. After five years in the original location, Lola bought the little bungalow on Third Avenue South and moved the business there, where it's been ever since.

Her husband helped her lay the linoleum floors, paint the walls, and generally transform the place from a one-family home into a house-of-beauty. These days the shop still reeks of 1958. The walls are blue, with pink-and-blue borders. The chairs and sinks look like they've been there for decades, although Lola has been through three generations of equipment, as well as customers.

A half-dozen chair hair dryers, including one so old that its massive helmet looks like something John Glenn wore during his famous Earth orbit in 1962, are scattered throughout the house. Tacked to the wall behind Gail's workstation is a Norman Rockwell calendar. On another wall, directly in her line of sight, is the tiny plaque Gail's husband bought at a mall crafts fair: "Beauticians don't retire—they just curl up and dye."

In a waiting area are a matching black vinyl couch, loveseat, and chair and a large box of Reese's Cups, peanuts, crackers, and other snacks for the ladies to munch on. In the back near the kitchen is a 1936 Coke machine that is Lola's pride and joy.

Despite the proliferation of walk-in franchise beauty shops and fancy style joints, and the increasing tendency of women to wash and dry their hair at home, Lola believes the institution of the beauty parlor remains alive and well. "Right now these girls are very, very busy, and that's the easy way out. They shampoo in the shower and blow it dry, and every damn one of 'em's late for work.

"The new beauty shops, with all the walk-ins, are very impersonal. In my estimation, you go not only to get yourself fixed but also to socialize. It's your time each week. These younger girls'll figure that out one day."

Like most old-time beauty parlors, the Beauty Box's bread-and-butter are the weekly shampoo-and-sets. Between permanents, women such as Mrs. Liner and Mrs. Hicks want their hair cleaned and curled and poofed once a week, and they don't want it to move much between visits.

"My daughter says, 'Mama, I can't understand why you don't wash your hair more often,'" Lola says. "I tell you what. I don't want to. It's not dirty, and I don't want to wash all the oil out. We can cut and blow dry, but our ladies don't want that. We try to keep our prices affordable for our retired people. But most of them have beaucoup money."

"I just love this business," says Lola. "It takes some artistic ability."

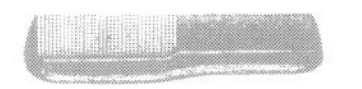

Because of the advancing age of so many of their customers, Lola and Gail sometimes have to be both beauticians and nurses. Two ladies have had strokes while sitting in their chairs. One with a bad heart collapsed on her way out the door. "We caught her before she hit the floor," Lola recalls. "I got her arms, and Gail got her feet, and we swung her onto the couch.

"She was turning blue, and Gail kept saying, 'She's dead, she's dead.'

"I said, 'Maybe not.' I got on the phone to call for help, and about that time she came to and said, 'Don't you call that ambulance.'"

At Gail's station, Mrs. Liner admires her freshly poofed raven hair, which looks stunning with her French manicure. She pays and waves good-bye to all the "girls."

In the back room Nettie, the manicurist, finishes up Jo Ann Nicholson and starts working on Ann Stephens. Mrs. Nicholson, a forty-six-year-old homemaker, and Mrs. Stephens, fifty-two, a high-school English teacher, are among the shop's youngest customers.

"I've been to lots of stylists, and my hair always dies in the middle of the week. Gail makes it last 'til I can get back," Mrs. Stephens says.

By late afternoon Lola puts the finishing touches on Margaret Warren's hair and announces she's finished for the day. She sweeps hair into a pile on the floor as Gail begins straightening up the curlers and brushes scattered around her station. Nettie reaches into the old Coke cooler and, drink in hand, heads out the door. Gail isn't far behind.

Lola, the last to leave for the day, searches for words to describe why, at age sixty-five and with the surrounding neighborhood increasingly plagued with inner-city problems, she'll be back tomorrow, tending to her ladies.

"I just love this business," she says. "It takes some artistic ability. And I prefer standing to sitting. Part of it is, you're producing a finished product. You see what you've accomplished. One of these days I'll retire. Our ladies are dying off, and I don't want to start over with another generation. When they're gone, I guess I'll be too." ■

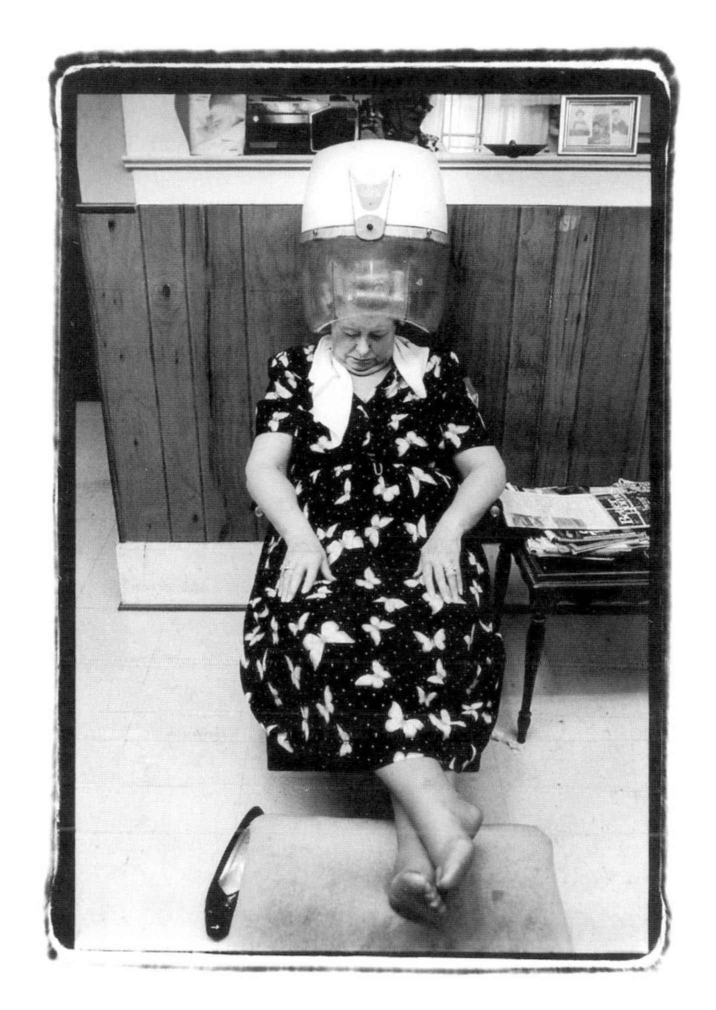

alabama rarely ranks at the top of America's Best–Of lists. When folks here talk about culture, oftentimes they mean football, barbecue, or Tammy Wynette, who, we're proud to report, was a beautician in Birmingham before heading up to Nashville for a career in country music. For all its shortcomings, though, Alabama surely ranks high when it comes to beauty parlors, which are almost as numerous as Baptist churches. And the names—they're hard to top. In Birmingham alone there are the Bee–Luv–Lee, the Beauteria, the Crown & Glory, and Johnnie's Beautyrama. Many owners, however, prefer a simpler moniker like Betty's Beauty Shop, in the state capital of Montgomery.

Betty's Beauty Shop

MONTGOMERY ALABAMA

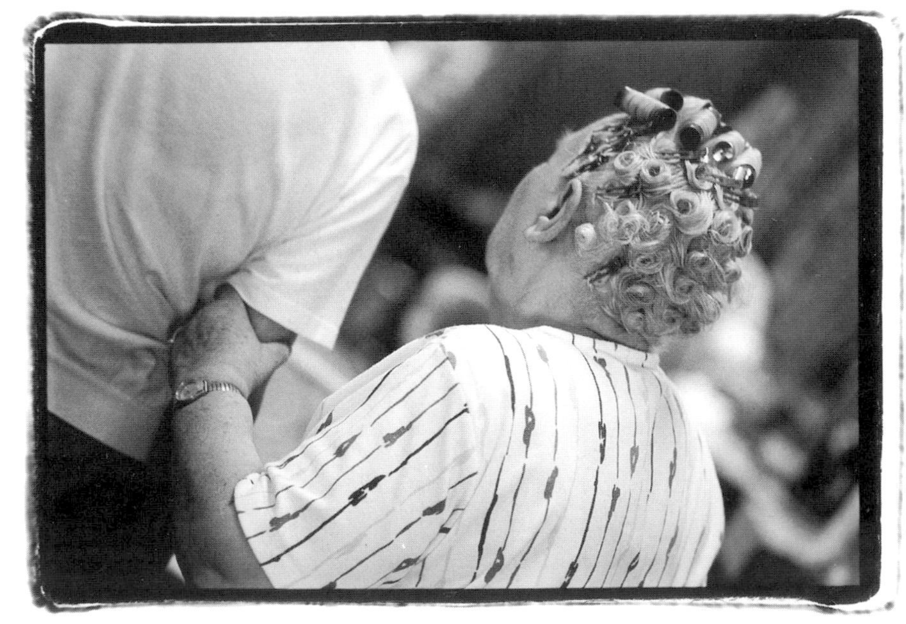

One lady (top) waits for her permanent to set while (bottom) a beautician leads a blind lady to a hair dryer.

At Betty's Beauty Shop beauticians work shoulder to shoulder, which may not allow for much elbow room but is a wonderful way to listen in on each other's conversations. In historic downtown Montgomery, not far from the site of fiery speeches by the Rev. Dr. Martin Luther King, Jr. and Gov. George Wallace, Betty's is a throwback to those long-ago days, even if the dryers and furniture have been updated. While the ladies are getting beautiful, they can read The National Enquirer *or rent a paperback for twenty-five cents.*

Broadway Beauty Shop

HOMEWOOD ALABAMA

In hoity-toity salons, smoking isn't allowed, which is not a bad idea considering the number of hairdos that used to go up in flames when a burning cigarette ignited hair spray. But at Broadway Beauty Shop in Homewood, Alabama, the rules can sometimes be lax. The ladies' lungs may get a bit tarnished, but their hair is clean, thanks to a weekly shampoo and a never-ending supply of sanitized brushes.

At Broadway Beauty customers aren't in a hurry to leave, even after their hair is fixed. That's because a good visit, a hearty laugh, and often a good-bye hug have long been part of the beauty-parlor experience. Typically the ladies would prefer death over going into the outside world before their beautifying is complete. But occasionally they have to run out to the car or run next door for a sandwich, to the feigned horror of the general populace.

PEPSI
BROADWAY BEAUTY SHOP
HAIR & NAIL CARE
Broadway
BEAUTY SHOP

Cinderella Beauty Shop

**MONTGOMERY
ALABAMA**

*At Cinderella Beauty Shop
the beauticians can't turn all their
customers into fairy princesses, but they
never let them leave looking like
wicked stepmothers.*

At Cinderella's, one of the oldest beauty shops in Alabama, this customer tries to squeeze in some reading as she gets rolled up. An hour later she smiles big at her weekly appointment's happy ending, if not her book's.

Joseph's Coiffeurs, Inc.

HOMEWOOD ALABAMA

Talk about your bad-hair day—or is that a beady-eyed squirrel on the lady's head? Actually it's a hairpiece in for a periodic poofing up at Joseph's Coiffeurs.

Pretty as a picture, complete with frame, is the way this customer looks after the magical ministrations of the Joseph's Coiffeurs beauticians.

Hair spray and hugs are what the ladies get at the end of a visit to Joseph's Coiffeurs. Here beauty isn't the sole province of the young—some beautiful older ladies also emerge from this place. And no one appreciates them more than their husbands, who often wait in the parking lot for the lovely apparitions to come strolling out the door.

SALLY
8.59

For three decades Mildred Strode has been beautifying women in a little shop in downtown Birmingham, just a few blocks from historic Kelly Ingram Park, where the Rev. Dr. Martin Luther King, Jr. led civil rights marchers in 1963. "I'm a beautician, advisor, and therapist," says Mrs. Strode, who refers to her customers as "rascals." Their favorite topic of conversation? "Men," Mrs. Strode says without hesitation. It's a subject that provides endless laughter in beauty shops across the South.

Patton's Beauty Shoppe

BIRMINGHAM ALABAMA

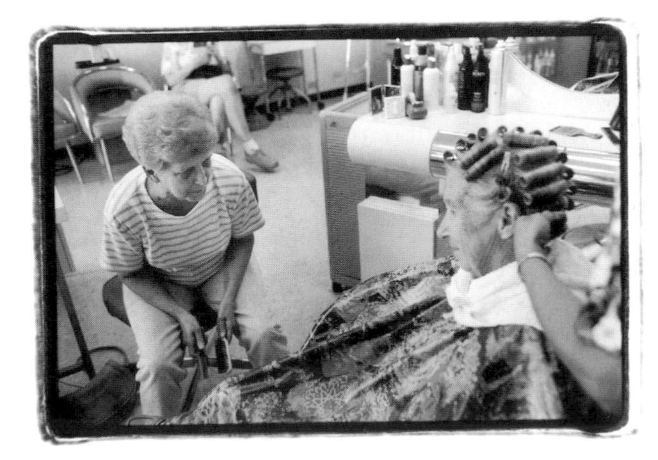

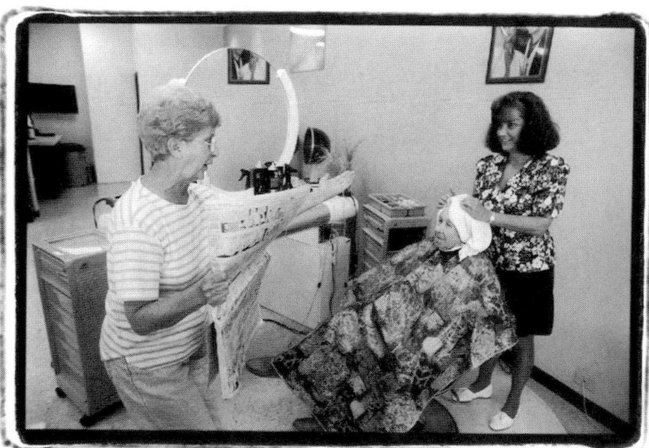

The Hair Parlor

FREEPORT
FLORIDA

Ralph Kline has this joke he likes to pull when his wife, Cherie, starts talking hair with her friends. He waits until just the right moment—after the women have touched on cuts, styles, and colors and are ready to launch into a Socratic-like dialogue on permanent waves—to announce innocently enough, "Cherie gave me my first permanent."

Ralph smiles sweetly and then, with unabashed glee, snatches off his straw hat, revealing a pate as shiny and smooth as a new bowling ball. "This here," he declares, "is about as permanent as it gets."

Cherie rolls her eyes and says, "Oh, Ralph," at which point he grins big and returns the hat to his head, covering up all but the dark, curly hair growing in a semicircle just above his ears. The illusion is almost magical.

Ralph performs this routine regularly at the diner next door to his wife's beauty shop, The Hair Parlor. At high noon nearly every day she puts the "Closed" sign on the shop's door and joins Ralph for lunch. He runs the metal recycling plant across the street in this rather unglamorous stop-in-the-road on the way south through the Florida panhandle to the coastal lights of Destin, Fort Walton Beach, and Panama City.

Cherie mesmerizes her ladies with horrific stories of hair fatalities she has witnessed.

Cherie opened The Hair Parlor a few years ago after working in a string of beauty shops along the Gulf Coast. She wanted her new business to resemble the sitting room of a Victorian mansion. With that in mind, she and Ralph painted the beauty shop bright pink outside, installed lace and antiques among the sinks and hair dryers, and christened the place with a name they thought would do the trick.

At age forty-seven, Cherie (pronounced Sharee) still has the looks and demeanor of the high-school cheerleader she once was. Blond and vivacious, with a squeally, girlish giggle, she can mesmerize audiences (i.e., her beauty shop ladies) with horrific stories of hair fatalities, which Cherie is happy to tell so long as the tales involve her only as a frightened witness.

"The worst catastrophe I've ever seen happened to one of my colleagues in beauty school," she says, her voice taking on a low and dangerous tone. "This lady came in with shoulder-length hair, highly bleached. She was in her late thirties, a very dressed-up, nice-looking lady, probably a secretary or something, and she came to the beauty school to get a perm.

"There was a young man, Butchy, who was doing her hair. We'd had instruction just the day before about doing perms on colored hair and the little treatments you're supposed to do while you do that.

"Well I was doing somebody else's hair in the next bowl, and I could look down and see his customer's head. Butchy was rinsing and talking, rinsing and talking, and I look down and see one of the lady's pink curlers just fall into the sink. Well I thought it had just come loose or something. Butchy rinses some more, and another curler falls into the sink, and I can see hair attached to it. I knew it wasn't supposed to do that."

Naturally Cherie pointed out the problem to Butchy, who, after much oh-dearing, ran off in search of the instructor.

"The teacher comes over and says, 'Oh my God! You've fried her hair!' The lady sits up and all these curlers fall out and she's got big patches of bald spots all over her head. She looks in the mirror and screams, and then I scream, and my customer sits up in the chair and screams, and we all just panic. I've never been able to get that picture out of my mind, of that hair and that scalp and all those people screaming. That's enough to make you be extra careful."

Cherie takes a long sip of her iced tea. Ralph starts fishing for another story. "Didn't one of y'all cut somebody's ear or something?" he asks his wife. This prompts the tragic tale of Debbie-the-Ripper, a young woman fresh out of beauty school, who worked with Cherie a few years back at a salon that also catered to men.

Debbie, as Cherie tells it, was cute and flirty and eager to trim every man who walked through the door. "Debbie was learning to do beards and mustaches, and she did a really neat job. She had a chair that would lay way back, and she'd rear 'em back and put the soft music on, butterin' 'em up for that big tip, you know."

Ralph's ears perk up. He suddenly interrupts. "How come you never let her do me?" he asks his wife. "Anyway," Cherie continues, ignoring him, "there was this guy come in, and Debbie was trimmin' him up, shaving him and everything, and all of a sudden we hear him go, 'OH! OH! OH-OH-OH!' Debbie was going, 'Oh my God!' I looked over and blood was every-where. On her, on him, just everywhere.

"My station was closest to hers, so I was the first one over. I said, 'What's the problem?' And I looked, and Debbie had

"She'd rear her men customers back and put the soft music on to butter 'em up."

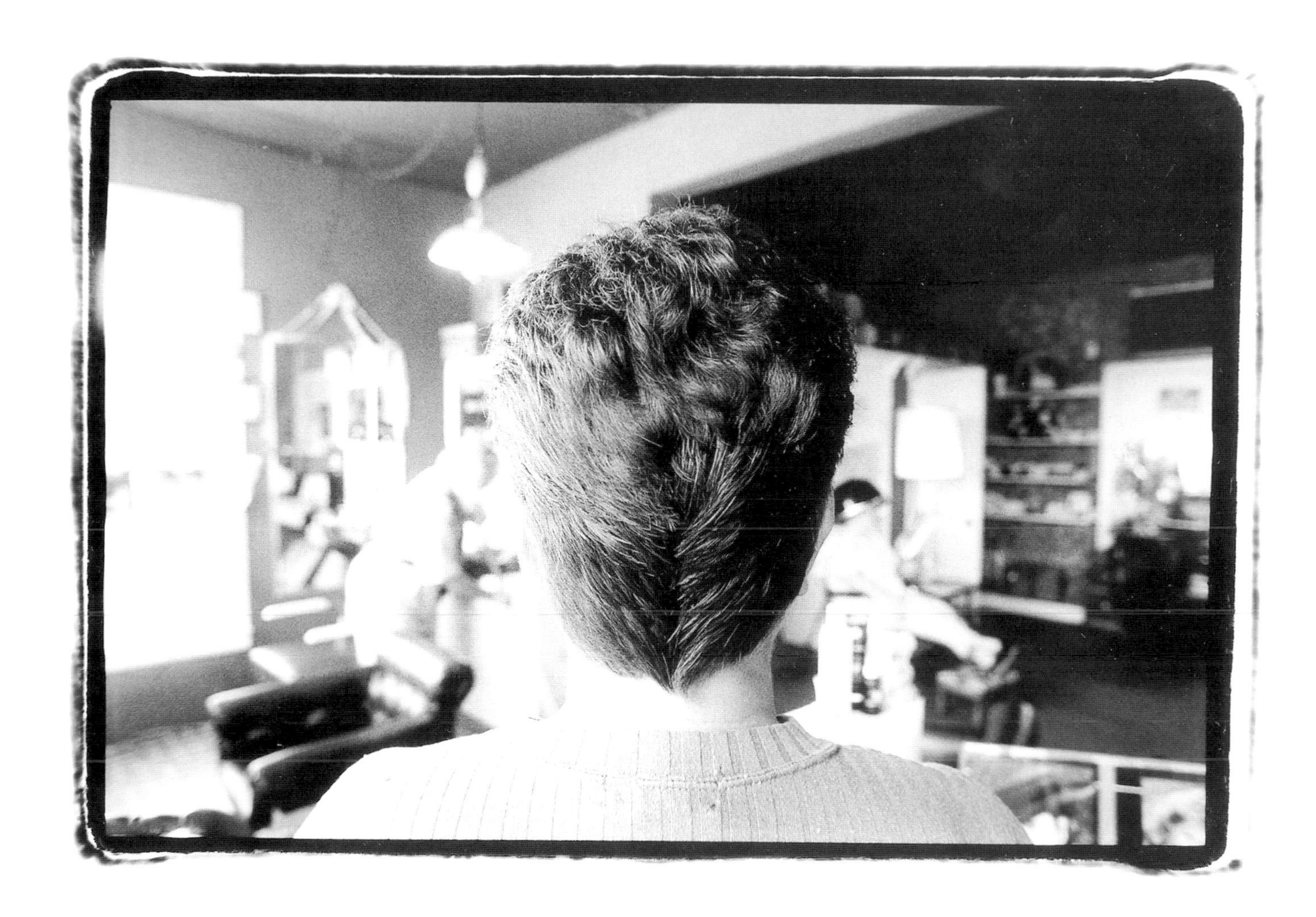

cut that middle thing in his nose, I don't know what you call it, but she just cut it right in two. I grabbed a towel and stuck it under there, and the hairdresser on the other side saw all that blood and had to sit down 'cause she was gonna faint. I said, 'Don't faint, we haven't got time to fool with you.' "

The last time Cherie saw the victim, he was departing with a "big ol' Band-Aid" under his nose. Needless to say, he left no tip. "I'm surprised he didn't sue," Cherie says.

Lunch ends on that note. Ralph says 'bye and heads back to the recycling plant. Cherie unlocks the door to The Hair Parlor, which is now open for business. Even though The Hair Parlor sits in the middle

of downtown Freeport, business doesn't exactly boom, although sometimes it does a kind of frisky tap dance across the carpeted floor. Cherie walks over to her delicately carved antique desk, decorated with silk roses and an antique reproduction telephone, and checks her appointment book. It being a Wednesday and downtown Freeport being little more than the main intersection of a well-traveled back road, business today is more like a slow ballet. So Cherie has time to offer a tour of the shop, where she is the owner, manager, and only beautician.

"I bought this from a little ol' lady who used to run a dress shop in town," Cherie says, pointing out a long wood-and-glass case full of shampoos, conditioners, and other beauty supplies. Cherie swears the display case is 150 years old. "I just love old things," she says, stopping beside a life-size metal mannequin outfitted in a long, pink, lace-trimmed dress that also dates back to the nineteenth century.

The shop's ceiling is painted green, and the walls are deep purple. A sitting area is outfitted in white wicker and photographs of Cherie's ancestors. "That old man is my granddaddy's uncle, with his wife, daughters, and their slave standing with them," Cherie says, lifting the picture off the wall for a close-up inspection. Another frame holds the picture of a dignified-looking black woman named Savannah Craig, photographed in 1885 on her wedding day. Savannah, Cherie says, was her grandmother's nanny.

Business doesn't exactly boom, but sometimes it does a kind of frisky tap dance across the carpeted floor.

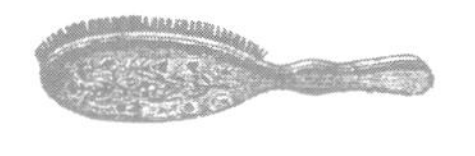

Cherie was born six hours north of Freeport in Birmingham, Alabama, to William and Lois Walker.

Her father, who was in the demolition business, moved his wife and seven children to Orlando, Florida, when Cherie was a child. Even then she had a flair for hair.

"I was curling and combing out my mother's hair when I was twelve. I'd tease it, do the whole thing. I'd give her perms, just following the instructions on the box. I'm sure it wasn't wonderful, but it suited her.

"My first job, you could say, was in the seventh grade. It was picture-taking day at school, and I'd snuck out a can of my mother's hair spray, and when it came time, I went in the bathroom and teased and fluffed up my hair and sprayed it. My girlfriend thought this was great and said, 'Do mine.' So I did hers. Well another girl came in and said, 'Do mine too,' and I said, 'Now I can't just keep using my mother's hair spray for free. Y'all are gonna have to pay.' They gave me ten cents apiece to tease and spray their hair. I had a pocketful of money."

Cherie and her girlfriends also discovered the beauty benefits of putting beer on their hair, which made it shine like a new coin. There were also unwelcome side effects. "We had to quit 'cause the flies got after us," she says.

For all her natural talent, Cherie had no childhood dreams of a career in hair. Her family eventually moved back to Birmingham, where she finished high school. One of her classmates was a boy in possession of a full head of thick dark hair, an impish grin, and the name Ralph Kline. He was a drummer in a band that often played along the Florida panhandle.

They didn't marry right away. Cherie's mother wanted her to go to Judson College, an all-female school in west Alabama. "I wasn't a bit interested in that," Cherie says.

"One day my girlfriend and I were downtown shopping, and we walked past this building called

The House of Beauty Beauty College. I didn't know anything about a beauty college. We walked in and started asking questions and I ended up registering, without even telling my mother."

Lois Walker, it turned out, was pleased enough to buy three $7 beautician's uniforms for her daughter's higher education. At the House of Beauty Beauty College, Cherie learned hair facts she'd never before considered. "You have to learn to see the problems when you see the scalp and head," she explains. "You've got to be able to see disease and know what it is, and whether it's contagious or not, and whether you need to send them to the doctor. We had classes on scalp diseases, nail diseases, perming, cutting, curling, coloring, the whole gamut."

Cherie learned to do a French twist, a beehive, and the highest high styles, such as a French twist with curls on top. She even invented a new do—with a side part, flat front, peaked back, and curls on the ears, like earmuffs.

"My favorite was the beehive. Very few people could do it. You had to have a lot of motion, a lot of arm work. I even had to stand on a Coca-Cola box behind one customer to do the top of it. It'd be from 6 to 8 inches taller than their heads. We'd put lacquer on it. That'd hold 'em for a week. And we recommended they wrap it in toilet paper and put a shower cap on top of it before they went to bed."

After graduating Cherie got a job doing high styling in a Birmingham shop run by twin sisters named Mel and Nell—Mel being the receptionist and Nell being the beautician. It was there, under the twins' tutelage, that Cherie witnessed the kind of beauty parlor episode that can only be repeated in a whisper and when no man, including her husband, is listening.

"There was this nerdy guy that used to come in that place. He had a crush on Gail, who was one of the other young hairdressers. Gail didn't like him. She said he had crud behind his ears. But he'd come in, and he'd say, 'You look so pretty, Gail.'

"One day she was cutting his hair, and he had his hands under his smock, and Gail looked down, and his smock seemed to be moving up and down. She screamed, 'You pervert!' and then whacked him in the lap with the hair dryer. And then she ran to the back room.

"He pulled out his hands, which were holding his broken glasses. He'd been cleaning them under the smock. He looked at us and kept saying, 'What'd I do? What'd I do?' "

One day Gail was cutting a man's hair, and he had his hands under his smock, and his smock seemed to be moving up and down. She called him a pervert and whacked him.

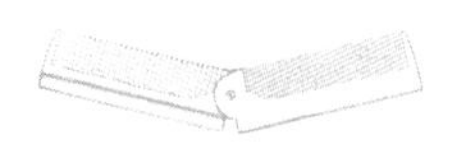

By then married to Ralph, Cherie stayed at that job until the birth of her first child, in 1968. The family moved briefly to Atlanta, and briefly back to Birmingham, before settling in Panama City, where Ralph was working long seasons with a band called Tyme.

As the family grew, Ralph went into the construction business, and Cherie did hair in a shop in Gulf Breeze, Florida, where she was an innocent bystander to yet another beauty mishap, this time involving one of that town's high-society matrons. The woman, a client of Cherie's, wore long hairpieces and frequently left them at the shop for Cherie to wash and style.

"I washed her little hairpiece one day, and I wrapped it up in a towel and left it laying in the back room on top of the washing machine to dry. I was supposed to have it all ready for her that afternoon at three o'clock. When I went back to work on it, I couldn't find the darn thing. Well we had a young man that worked for us, and it was his day to do all the laundry. And it turns out that he had bunched up all the towels and thrown 'em in the washer, and he had washed her hairpiece and dried it with the towels.

"When I found it, that thing was wadded up into a tight, tangled-up, matted fur ball. And she's coming in at three o'clock. I just panicked. The owner of the salon called her and said, 'Your hairpiece is just not going to be ready by three so could you come in tomorrow?' And then we got on the phone and started calling the hair hotlines."

One hair crisis counselor finally came up with a solution: Spray the thing with water and baking soda. By midnight Cherie had combed out the tangles. The next day the unsuspecting society matron walked out of the shop wearing her machine-washed, tumble-dried hair, and another lawsuit was avoided.

Another of Cherie's Gulf Breeze clients was Ed Walters, who became internationally famous in the late 1980s for his homemade videotapes of a UFO. He later became even more internationally famous when some spoilsport found what looked an awful lot

like the videotaped UFO under the insulation in Walters's attic.

"I cut Ed's hair, and I also did his wife's hair," Cherie says. "All that UFO stuff was real controversial. They tried to say he made it up. But I don't think he did. I knew him personally, and he wasn't that type. I think somebody just wanted it to look that way."

Cutting Ed Walters's hair was not the extent of Cherie's involvement with UFOs. "We saw one," she announces. "During the time when they were having all those UFO sightings down here, we saw something we couldn't identify."

She acknowledges that some of those once-stylish dos she was so good at creating, in particular the beehive, could, at a distance, make even the most attractive woman look like a creature from outer space. But there's no time to reflect on that now. Cherie's first customer of the afternoon, an elderly woman named Helen, has just walked in for her weekly wash-and-set.

Helen settles into the shampoo chair and delivers a traffic report. "That flatbed trailer just ran right over that pickup truck," she tells Cherie. "I didn't see it happen, but I drove right by it."

Cherie is appropriately horrified, and then inquires about Helen's husband, who, after dropping her off at The Hair Parlor, has gone next door for coffee. "When I first started hairdressing, men wouldn't dare enter a beauty shop," Cherie says. "Helen's husband is still kind of that way. He gets his hair cut at the barber shop.

"But I get men in here. I think they are much more vain about their looks than women are. They want it combed just right, with gel, all that stuff. I've noticed with my brothers and sons that they spend more time in front of that mirror, combing their little hairs.

"I have a young man with real long hair who comes in to get it trimmed, and he's a nervous wreck. He'll let me cut a little, and then he wants to look. When he leaves, you'd never know he's had a haircut."

Hair curled-up tight, Helen takes a seat under the dryer. She hangs her large white purse on the arm of the dryer chair and cools her reddening face with a cardboard fan bearing a picture of Jesus. Meanwhile a young, blond woman arrives for her appointment. She's a semiregular, Cherie confides. The young woman, who appears to be recovering from a bad perm, says, "Trim it, but try not to take any off the length."

With her scissors open in her hand, Cherie takes a second or two to digest those instructions. "What?" she finally asks. Once the appropriate cut-but-not-cut style is agreed upon, Cherie acknowledges that she's beginning to understand why ladies of a certain age, like Helen, wash their hair only once a week.

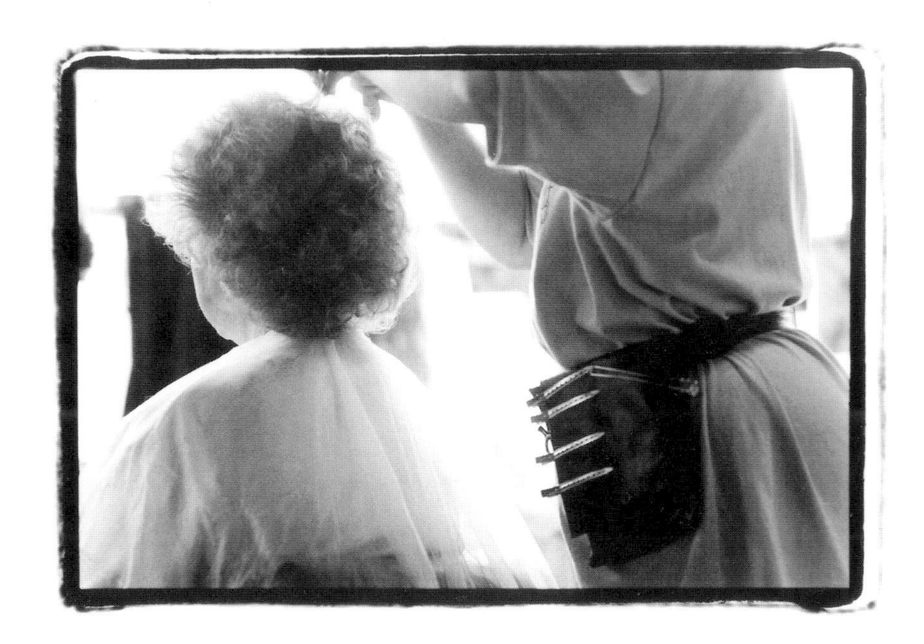

"You can do just so many styles, and then you have to start over. Remember the Farrah Fawcett cut, where it all was blown back? Well the cuts on *Friends* are the same except it's all blown forward. Dorothy Hamill's wedge cut, back in the seventies, was a modified Beatles cut. Now the girls are wearing a softer, smoother look, like the 1920s. I'm just glad they're getting rid of those bumper bangs."

The telephone jingles. Cherie picks it up and says, "Hair Parlor." It's one of her regular wash-and-set ladies calling to change her appointment. The transaction takes a full five minutes. "I had to hear about her whole life," Cherie says when she hangs up. "She can't get over that wreck that happened yesterday."

Helen, now dry, returns to the styling chair for Cherie to comb her out. Helen tells Cherie that beer is good for hair. "You put beer on your hair?" Cherie asks her. The older woman shakes her head. "No, but I drink a little," she says.

By 4 p.m. a few more customers have come and gone. Sara Rexroad, who works for the Freeport Tourist Bureau, is sitting in Cherie's chair, getting her hair curled with a hot iron. That effort is not so much to curl her red hair as to straighten it a bit. "It'd be an Afro if I let it go natural," Ms. Rexroad says.

"As ladies get older, their skin starts drying out. Everything starts drying out. Their scalp doesn't get as oily and dirty as younger ladies' do. And they're not as active as we are, so they don't get the dust and dirt that we do. I wash my hair every day. But I've got to the point where mine's starting to dry out. Now I can go two days without washing it."

Cherie's straight hair almost touches her shoulders. She gets it trimmed every month or so, but that's the extent of her personal beautifying. She used to wear it fancier, but raising her three children plus three foster kids meant less time in front of the mirror.

In nearly thirty years of professional hair-doin', she's seen prices go up and styles come back around.

"I usually come in once a week and get it curled 'cause I just can't do anything with it. Sometimes if I'm real nice, Cherie will even massage my neck."

Cherie, by the way, is wearing what looks like a construction worker's tool belt, except that in place of hammers and screwdrivers, her belt holds clips, combs, brushes, and scissors. Cherie performs most cuts with a $265 pair of sheers that not only are sharp enough to shave a man but also have a lifetime guarantee from the manufacturer.

She likes to offer little extras for her clients. Once a year she holds a "glamor shots" day, where for a modest fee she fancies up the ladies' hair, clothes, and makeup and has a photographer take their pictures in soft, gauzy lighting. "That's made me popular in this town," Cherie says. "Last year we did twenty-five ladies. We make 'em look good. Sometimes it's not easy. We had to use the hot wax to make a space between one woman's eyebrows."

Cherie is hoping she'll soon have another service to offer: manicures. She already has a girl lined up for the job as soon as she gets out of beauty school. Speaking of manicures, Cherie has one more horror story to tell from her days in Gulf Breeze.

"We had this lady who came and got her nails done every week. Every now and then she'd have the sculptured nails put on. Well the nail technician had a bowl of acetone sitting there that you soak the nails off with. And this old lady, she was real shaky anyway, she turned her lighter on to light a cigarette, and she dropped that lighter in that bowl of acetone, and fire shot up right through that lady's hair and onto the curtains.

"The lady wasn't hurt—just singed, mostly. They just passed a law a couple of years ago that says no smoking in beauty shops, except in designated areas. I make my ladies go outside. You just can't be too careful." ■

Cherie holds a "glamor shots" day, where she fancies up her ladies' hair, clothes, and makeup and has a photog-rapher take their pictures in soft, gauzy lighting.

Even though much of the nation's Southern-most state seems like an extension of New York City or Havana, Cuba, there is one tiny area at the top of the peninsula that remains pure Deep South. In the Florida panhandle, just below the state lines of Alabama and Georgia, you'll find an abundance of barbecue joints, trailer parks, big girls and big-girl hair and fabulous beauty parlors. One of the most colorful is Mae's Beauty Shop, in the panhandle town of Red Bay, run by Mae Chamberlin (at right) who entertains clients by playing hymns on her organ between wash-and-curls jobs and permanent waves. When Mae finishes her day's work, she doesn't have a long drive home. Her shop is attached to her house.

Mae's Beauty Shop

RED BAY
FLORIDA

Inside Mae's Beauty Shop beautician and organist Mae Chamberlin, age sixty-six, talks as fast as she rolls, and customers are free to tune in–or out– as they see fit. Most tune in, as Mae's small talk is too good to miss.

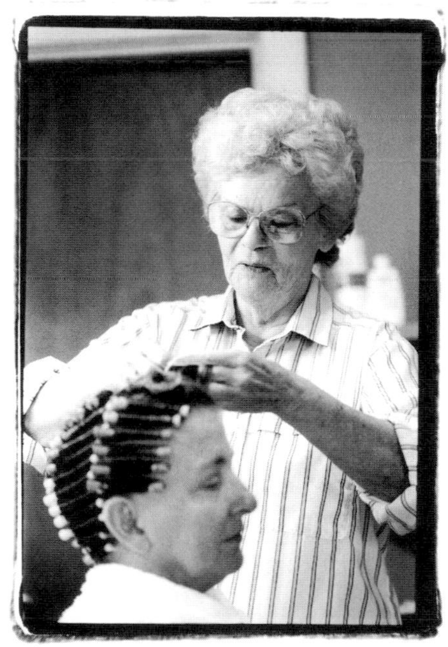

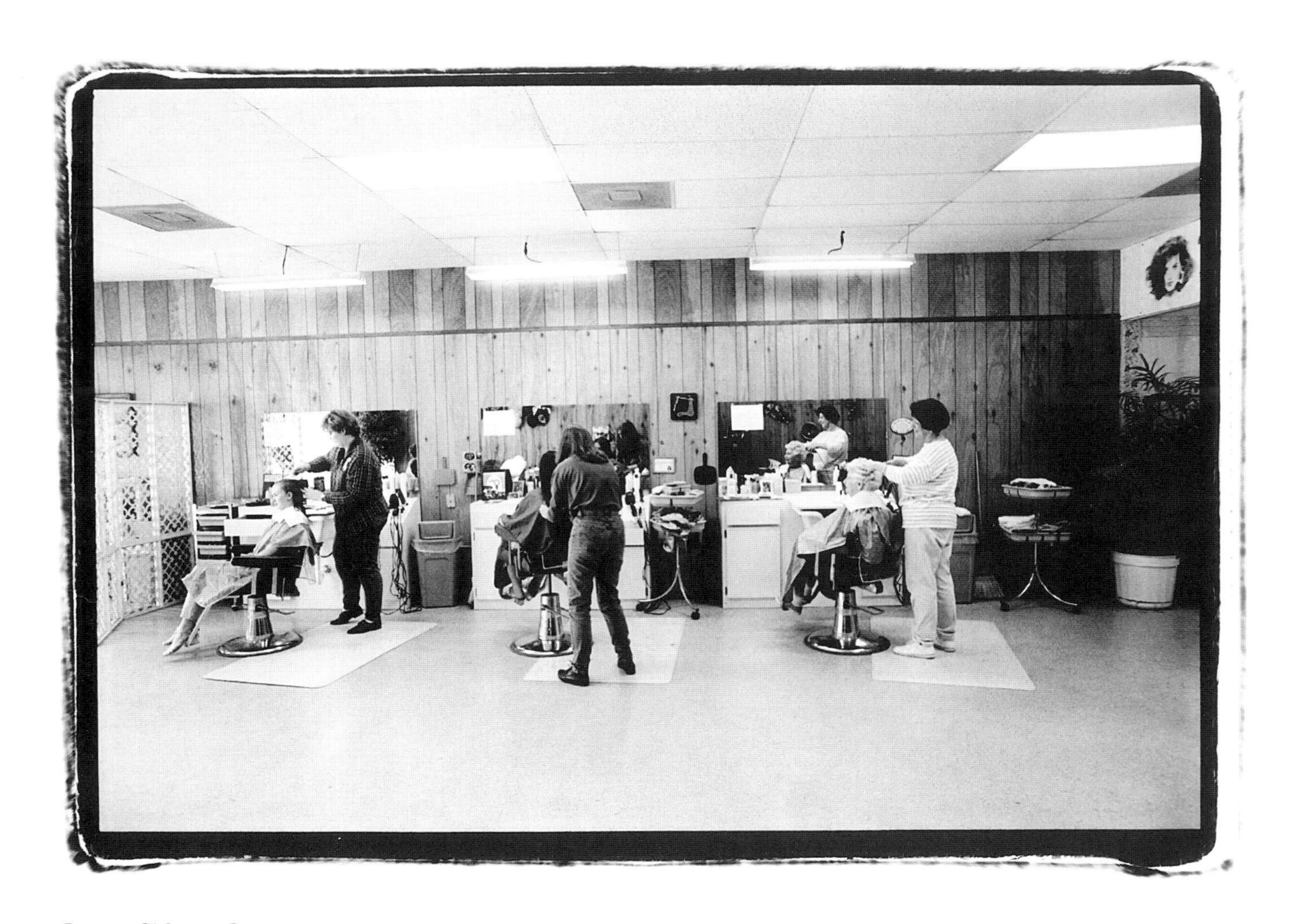

Ann's Hair Designs

DEFUNIAK SPRINGS
FLORIDA

At Ann's Hair Designs a trio of beauticians makes magic with customers at three identical stations in the large, paneled room.

Inside Ann's Hair Designs beautician and thirty-three-year-veteran shop owner Ann Bird puts the finishing touches on one longtime customer and then gets a hug from another emerging from under the dryer. If Ann appears to be enjoying her job, that's because she is. And, as her coffee mug suggests, she'd like her customers to love their hairstylist as much as she loves her job.

Hair Designs by Sherry

FREEPORT FLORIDA

While waiting for his wife to get beautified inside Hair Designs by Sherry, this husband covers his eyes with his baseball cap and enjoys a nap, which is a procedure many men believe makes them more beautiful. Inside the shop, beautician Sherry Edwards is hard at work, surrounded by wet heads and curling utensils.

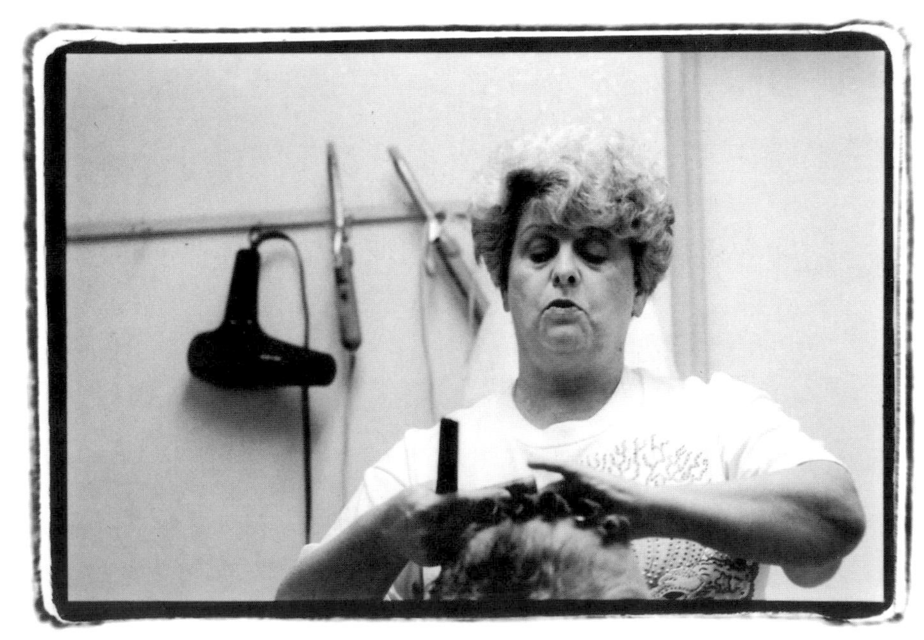

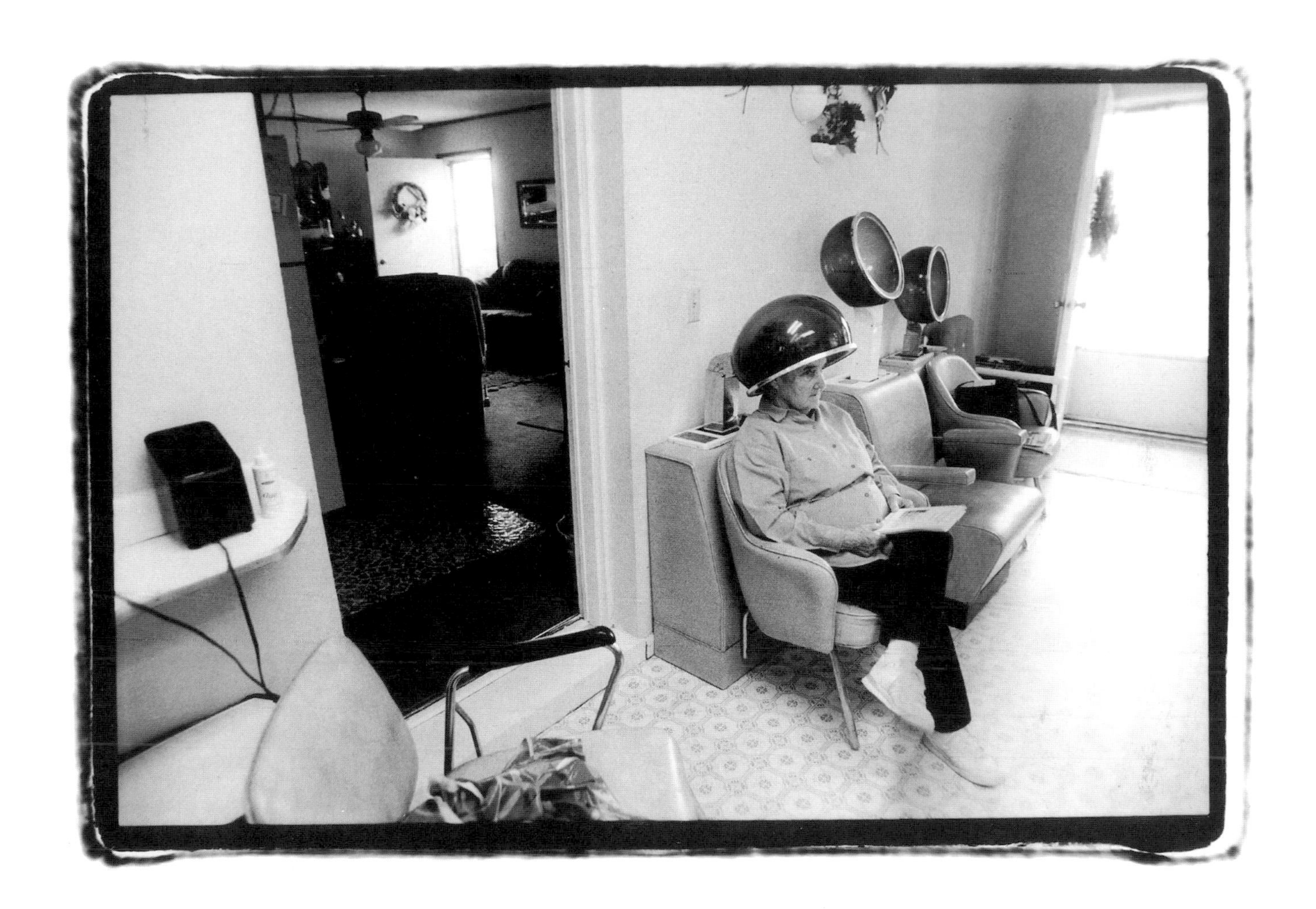

Gertrude Jackson gets a Florida sunshine bath as she waits for the bell to ring on the hair dryer at Hair Designs by Sherry, which is inside Sherry Edward's home.

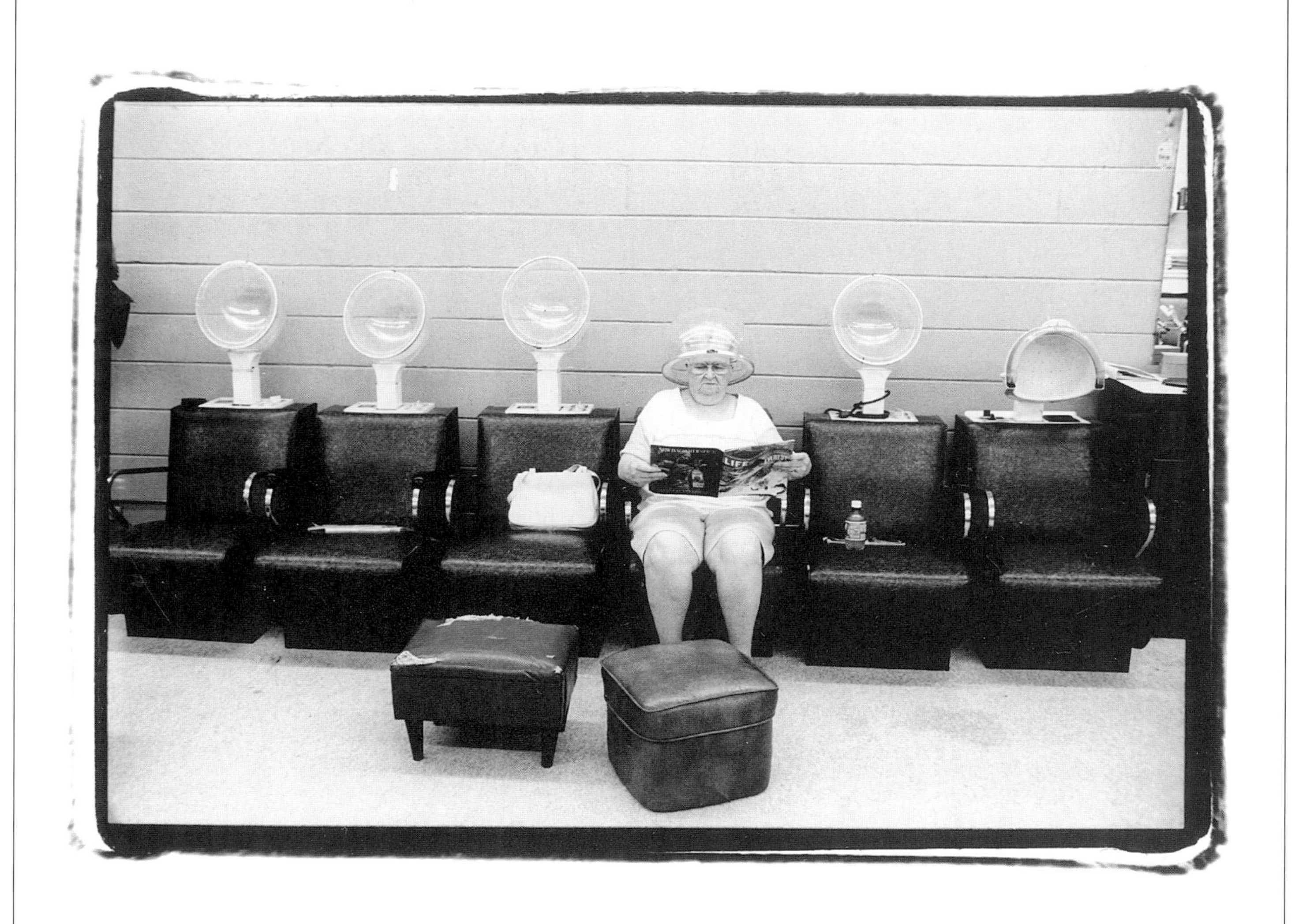

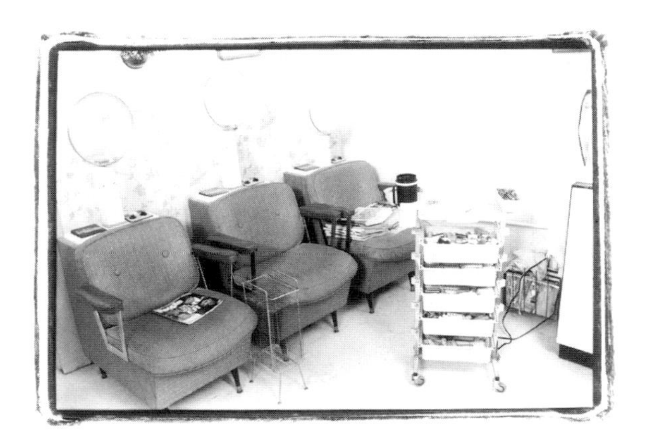

Babette's Cut & Curl

■

DOUGLASVILLE
GEORGIA

With country music blaring from the radio and a deaf and blind cockapoo dog underfoot, Babette Pritchard lifts a swatch of Buddy Truitt's gray hair and scissors away a quarter-inch of split ends.

She trims the left side, the right side, and finally the top. Then, with cutting instrument still in hand, she walks behind her customer to smooth out his remaining scraggly ends. Just as she gets within a short stabbing distance of Truitt's neck, the beautician trips, launching the scissors like a heart-seeking missile across the small beauty parlor.

"Dammit to hell, Phoebe!" Babette snaps at the eighteen-year-old dog, whose cloudy eyes haven't seen a thing. Babette bends down to pick up the scissors. Regaining her balance and, eventually, her pride, she instructs her assistant, Tiffany Armour, to keep the animal well out of her way.

"I think it's about time to be putting her to sleep," Babette announces, meaning the dog, not the assistant. Besides being old and generally infirm, Phoebe has cancer. When she's not getting tangled in Babette's feet, the dog is throwing up from her medication. "Phoebe smells so bad now I can't hardly stand it," the beautician declares. "My house stinks, my car stinks, and now this place is starting to stink."

"What all colors have you dyed that dog?" Marshall asks. "Lord, she's been every kind of color there is," replies Babette.

Tiffany rolls her eyes and shakes her head. Truitt smiles. Longtime customer Linda Farrar, whose fifteen-year-old son, John, is waiting for a haircut, softly asks how long the beautician has owned little Phoebe, who now seems to be pondering a run toward the door.

"Oh, Lord, she's been with me forever," Babette says in her raspy drawl, a souvenir from years of cigarettes. When she quit smoking, so did her customers, at least while they're in Babette's little downtown shop. A sign posted dead center on the mirror reads, in large black ominous letters, "No smoking or soliciting." And when Babette or her signs say something, they mean it.

Yet for all her gruff talk, the forty-five-year-old owner and sole operator of Babette's Cut & Curl is, deep down, as soft-hearted as they come as long as you don't make her mad. "I seriously doubt if she'll ever have that dog put to sleep," whispers Nelson Marshall, a local lawyer and longtime customer, when Babette is out of earshot. "I just don't think she could do it."

From his office down the street, Marshall, fifty-five, has wandered in to ask Babette if she could work him in later for a haircut. It being lunch hour, however, he sticks around a while to shoot the breeze.

"What all colors have you dyed that dog?" Marshall asks, looking at the curly-haired blond critter now sleeping on the floor. Babette laughs. "Lord, she's been every kind of color there is. Purple, pink, blue, red. I gave her a mohawk when the Braves were winning. Phoebe's my best customer."

On this particular Saturday, Babette's too

busy to give Phoebe a wash-and-wag. She has two customers under the dryers, one in the styling chair, and several more waiting for her magical ministrations. An impressive number are middle-aged men, who claim to be drawn by Babette's barbering expertise but don't seem to mind that she's blond, petite, bosomy, and fond of wearing tight-fitting, lacy tops.

Today she wears a black peekaboo affair, sheer enough in the back to reveal a bra strap in shocking purple. Her jeans are bell bottoms, circa 1973. Her long blond curls, almost identical in color to

Phoebe's, are piled high on her head, with tendrils framing her eternally tanned face. The overall effect suggests a trailer-park Ivana Trump.

Babette's bridgework, by the way, sits on the front desk, next to her appointment pad. "It was hurting my gums," she explains without a hint of embarrassment. Although her customers include some of the town's loveliest ladies, Babette doesn't edit her life or her language, which generally includes a cussword every other sentence. Her customers all know, usually after the first visit, that she's been divorced six times and got hauled off to jail a few years back for fighting with her sister.

In this rather slow-moving town of about 12,000, Babette's colorful life offers more entertainment than anything to be found thirty minutes away on Interstate 20 in Atlanta.

"Babette is extremely interesting," declares Truitt, fifty-nine, a local insurance agent. "Back in my younger days, I'd eat dirt and die 'fore I'd come in a beauty shop. Then I decided a woman's hands are softer than a man's. Plus, I like Babette. She cuts hair good, and she knows everybody and everything. She can tell you to go to hell and make you look forward to the trip."

"I like Babette. She cuts hair good, and she knows everybody and everything."

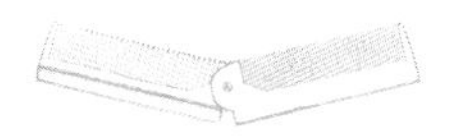

"That's right," Babette snaps, whacking Truitt playfully upside his newly trimmed head. In no hurry to pay or leave, Truitt crosses his arms and leans against the wall, hoping to hear a bit of news.

Settling yet another male customer into the styling chair, Babette announces that a string of popular restaurants named Babette's has caused her some difficulty. "You know they opened one of those in Atlanta, and people are always calling me to make reservations," she says. "Maybe I should start serving some food. Tiffany, will you make me a banana sandwich?"

Dutifully the assistant heads out the door to a nearby grocery for a loaf of bread and a jar of mayonnaise. While she's gone, the beauty parlor crowd debates whether Elvis preferred peanut butter or mayonnaise on his legendary banana sandwiches.

"Mayonnaise," Babette says with authority. "I heard he used both," somebody else offers in a can-you-believe-it tone.

Former Douglasville mayor and longtime pharmacist Gwynne Maurer, sixty-one, saunters in to join the noontime conversation. He and Truitt are soon recapping their favorite story. It concerns an unfortunate black man who visited Maurer's drugstore wearing a turtleneck sweater pulled over his mouth. "We thought he was robbing the place," Maurer says, as Truitt eggs him on. It seems the pharmacist didn't wait to see what the turtleneck-wearing customer wanted. He let out a yell and dialed the police as other customers began to panic.

"The police got on him in a second," Maurer says. "Turns out he'd been to the dentist that morning to have a tooth pulled and was coming in to get his prescription. It was cold outside, and he was trying to keep his mouth warm so it wouldn't hurt so bad.

"My mother could lay down and roll on the floor, and her hair wouldn't move."

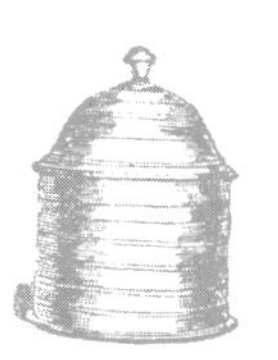

"Funniest thing about it was, everybody in that store had pulled out a gun, thinking this guy was a robber. It was the heaviest armed bunch of folks you've ever seen. Scared that man to death. He never came back."

After having listened to this story a few hundred times, Babette is in no mood to laugh. She's consulting with young John Farrar, who wears his dark hair nearly shaved on the sides and a tad longer on top. His most distinguishing feature is his long, dark sideburns, which he entrusts only to Babette. "She does it right," Farrar says. "You go to one of these new places, and they want to cut my sideburns off."

Farrar is a third-generation customer at Babette's Cut & Curl. His mother, Linda, is a regular, as is Linda's mother, "Miss Willie" McEaddy, who comes every week for a wash-and-set. "She's one of my starch-and-irons," Babette says of Miss Willie. Linda Farrar nods from her seat near the door. "My mother could lay down and roll on the floor, and her hair wouldn't move."

"I do too many of them wash-and-curls," Babette says. "They take too long to do and the money's not good. But you can't get rid of 'em. When this generation dies off, I think the younger women are going to start wanting the same thing, once a week. Otherwise they're gonna go bald from washing their hair so much."

As soon as the ex-mayor and the insurance agent leave, Babette is ready to gossip. "Buddy just got his second divorce," she says of the affable Truitt. "While he was going through that, I heard more than his psychiatrist did, if he had one."

She launches into a discussion of her various male customers' wives. The way Babette tells it, every middle-aged man in town has ditched a caring, middle-aged wife for a pretty, young semi-floozy. "Babette knows all the gossip," Linda Farrar says appreciatively.

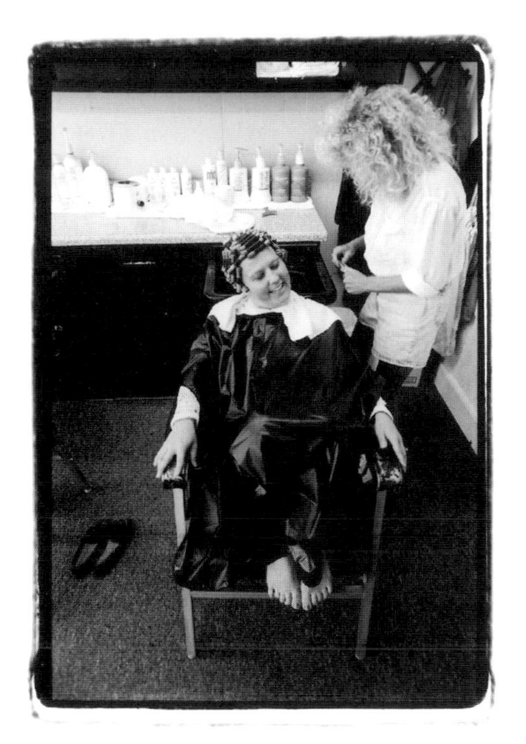

"I've been to these chain shops, and it's just not the same," Mrs. Farrar continues. "They don't know your hair, they don't know your history, they don't know you. It's just not as interesting."

Babette nods. "And they don't give you their home phone number so you can call 'em when you need 'em," she says.

Before she can elaborate, customer Helen Stacey, sixty-two, arrives for her weekly wash-and-set.

Babette tells her not to leave without the blue Tupperware bowl she brought in last week full of soup for the beautician. Tiffany, back from the grocery, shampoos Mrs. Stacey, who has been a customer of Babette's for nearly thirty years.

"I first met Babette when she was working at Cleo's," Mrs. Stacey says. "She was just a teenager, but she had a natural knack for doing hair. She's a born beautician. It came natural to her, and it showed."

Mrs. Stacey recalls the teenage Babette as "a little floozy, a little tiny floozy. She seemed like a fun-loving teenager, but she had the responsibilities of an older person. She was one of the few around here who knew how to tease. She started giving me a little bouffant, but not the really high stuff. From that we went to platinum blond. When I got allergic to bleach, she figured out a way to keep me blond without bleach. She'd give me all these glamorous hairdos, with hairpieces and braids and French twists and all sorts of stuff. For a while, she had me looking like Kim Novak. I wasn't going anywhere special. Women back then were just more glamorous.

"I knew all her husbands," Mrs. Stacey continues. "When my Mama died, Babette did her face and hair. She was ninety-two years old and didn't have a wrinkle in her face. Babette made her look so beautiful."

More than any of Babette's customers, Mrs. Stacey understands what makes her tick. She's seen the beautician through six marriages and divorces, the stabbing death of her brother, and the kind of horrific tragedy that makes a young woman grow up fast.

"When her boy got killed, that liked to killed all of us," Mrs. Stacey says. "Babette had her beauty shop in her home then, and the little thing was sitting on

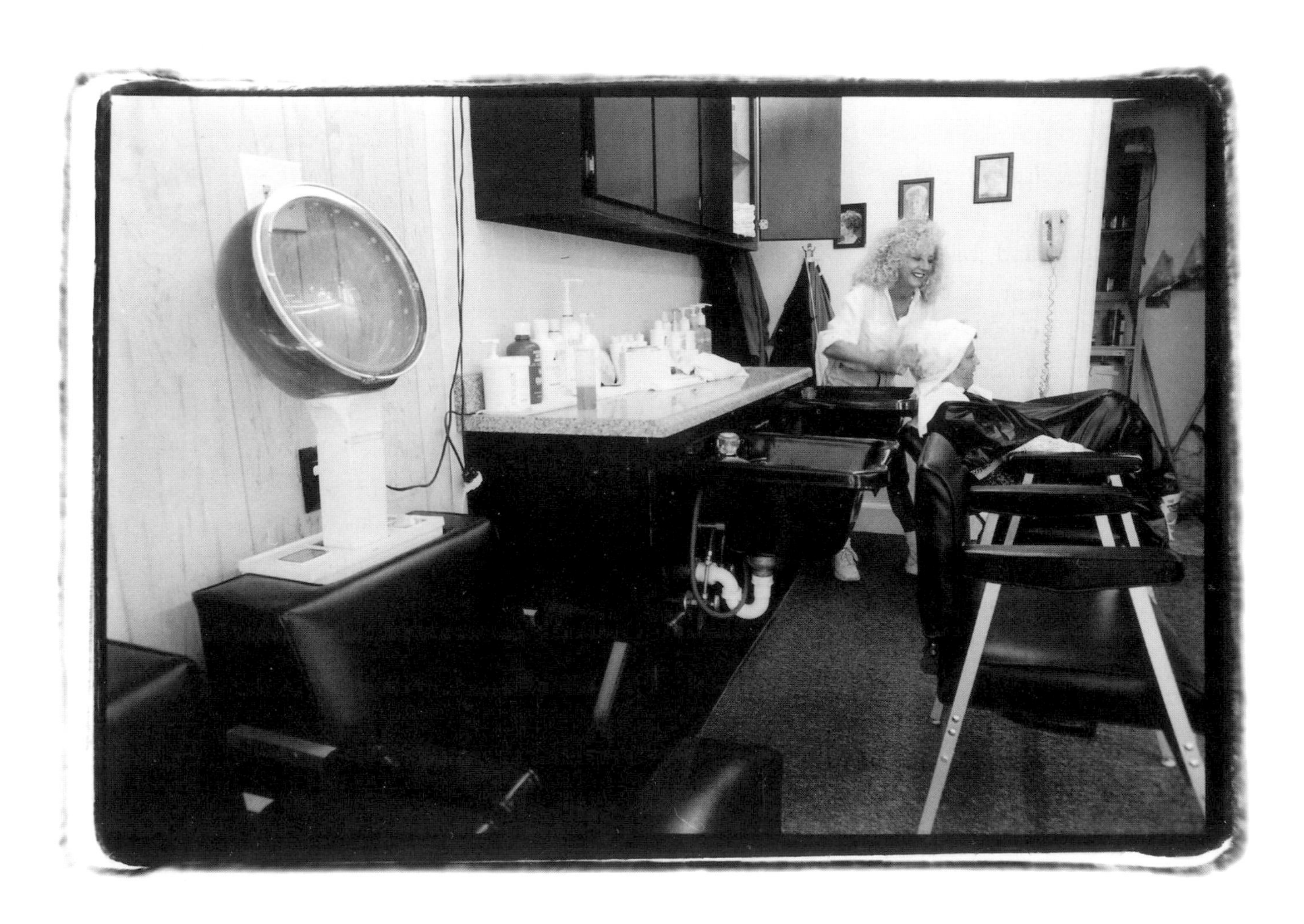

the curb when a car came up on the curb and killed him. We've shared happy times and sad times, and that was the saddest of all."

Babette's only child, Jackie, was five years old when he was killed in 1979. To this day, she has a hard time talking about the accident. "Life goes on" is what she usually says when the subject comes up.

"I think doin' hair kind of runs in my family," says Babette. "I started doin' my mother's hair when I was ten."

Her son's death was a singular blow in a life filled with hard times. Born and raised in nearby Tallapoosa, Georgia, Babette lived with her father, Marshall Brown, a disabled veteran, and her mother, Agnes, who stayed home to take care of six children. In school Babette was a scrappy little girl called Bo Bo. "The kids couldn't say Babette," she explains.

One of her childhood buddies, Rhubarb Jones, now a popular radio personality in Atlanta, reminisced in a recent column in his hometown newspaper about growing up in the country with Bo Bo. "She could ride a two-wheeler since she was three," Jones wrote. "I could not be outdone by Bo Bo Brown, who could beat up any boy in the first grade."

At thirteen Babette got a job as a shampoo girl in the Gala Beauty Shop on the main drag in Tallapoosa. Two years later she dropped out of high school and lied about her age to get into beauty school. By eighteen she was a licensed, full-time beautician.

"I think doin' hair kind of runs in my family," she says. "My daddy had two brothers who were barbers, and their daughters were beauticians. I started doin' my mother's hair when I was ten. Me and my sisters, we all worked on her. My mother had no talent with hair."

In Tallapoosa in the late 1960s, the main source of entertainment for teenagers was impromptu drag races through the middle of town. "There wasn't nothin' to do 'cept drinkin', shootin', and drivin'," Babette says. "Sometimes we'd go to the dirty movies at the Peachtree Theater in Atlanta."

In her early days as a beautician, Babette did beehives and finger curls and the occasional geometric Sassoon cut. By then she'd married a young man who gave her a son and the last name she'd keep through five more marriages and divorces. "Most of 'em didn't last but a year or two," Babette says. "Mamaw thinks I ought to have a husband reunion."

Mamaw, the name everybody calls the elderly woman who has just arrived, harrumphs at that notion. She sits down to wait for her shampoo. Tiffany, meanwhile, has finally delivered Babette's

banana sandwich, and the beautician scarfs it down without bothering to reinstall her dental accessory.

Through the 1970s and '80s, Babette changed husbands more often than she changed beauty shops. One husband was an accountant. Another worked in construction. There was a landscaper, a handyman, and, alas, a mortician. "First date I had with him, we embalmed a body," Babette says enthusiastically. "I watched him do it right there in the funeral home."

Babette stops talking when a dark-haired young man in black jeans and a black T-shirt walks in. He meets with her in a conference of whispers and then leaves with Phoebe the dog in tow. "That's Victor," Babette says when the door closes after them. "He thinks he's my boyfriend.

"I don't go lookin' for men. They find me. Victor may be here today, gone tomorrow. There's been a bunch of 'em. I found out there's no such thing as love. It's like gas. It passes on."

Yet the men keep coming—some, ostensibly, for a haircut. While Babette rolls Mamaw's short gray hair, in walks lawyer Marshall, returning for his haircut, and postal worker John Baker, fifty, who rode right up to the Cut & Curl's front door on a Suzuki motorcycle.

The men talk to each other as Babette finishes Mamaw and then puts color on Mrs. Stacey, who tells her, "Don't forget my front porch." Front porch, Babette explains, is what Mrs. Stacey calls her dark roots.

The older woman talks about a friend who's in the hospital and claims to be starving to death. "I want you to know, they won't feed her," Mrs. Stacey tells Babette. "I had to cook her something to eat and carry it up there. I've never heard of a hospital like that."

"I had to go up there the other night with my allergies," Babette says. "It was $50 right then, and when the bill came, it was another $400."

Marshall walks over to listen to the women talk. He prefers a beauty parlor over a barber shop, he says, in part because of the quality of the conversation. "Men talk about things—guns, cars, jobs, raises. You always feel like you have to compete. In here, the ladies talk about ideas and people. You find out a lot of useful information. Several times, stuff I've picked up in here I've used in court."

Working in front of the plate-glass window, the sun washing over her, Babette starts to sweat. "Open that door," she instructs Tiffany, who props the front door open with a brick. After rinsing Mrs. Stacey, Babette tells Baker, the postal worker, to have a seat in the styling chair. He immediately starts complaining about his job.

"Mismanagement is behind the postal situation," declares Baker, a steward in the postal workers union. "Most people are overqualified. There's a lot of frustration and boredom. The only place they don't have a camera to watch you is in the bathroom."

"You don't ever hear about a beautician pulling a gun and killing everybody," Babette says, smiling. She walks over to her desk, reaches into a drawer, and pulls out a holstered .32 pistol, to demonstrate, perhaps, that it's still a possibility.

With that display, the conversation veers into a rundown of what sounds like a full-fledged crime

wave in Mayberryesque Douglasville. "The drugstore on the corner just got robbed," Babette says. "And the police station is right there across the street. They try something like that with me and I'll make 'em regret it. I still like a good fight." ■

You might think, in the wake of the 1996 Centennial Olympic Games in Atlanta, that Georgia folks have grown a bit uppity, in attitude and personal style. And while this is true to some extent (just visit the elegant salons in Atlanta's Buckhead neighborhood, for example), most of your diehard, kiss-my-grits Georgia gals remain as downhome as peach cobbler on Saturday night. Inside the Alpharetta Beauty Shop north of Atlanta, the ladies are itching to keep up with the goings-on in the world, which is why they sit under the hair dryers with a stack of papers generally consisting of such international fountains of journalism as *The National Enquirer*, the *Globe*, and the *Sun*.

Alpharetta Beauty Shop

ALPHARETTA GEORGIA

Occasionally, in the midst of beautifying one customer, Alpharetta Beauty Shop hairdoer Martha Collett will stop what she's doing to ask the opinion of another customer because, as every Southern woman knows, you can never have too many opinions on how to be beautiful.

Chatter Box Hair Salon

LITHIA SPRINGS
GEORGIA

Inside the Chatter Box Hair Salon in Lithia Springs just west of Atlanta, customers can choose from a wide variety of beauty products, seemingly endorsed by Marilyn Monroe, the most beautiful of them all. Another poster celebrates the old-fashioned glories of Wildroot Cream-Oil for men, who, in the olden days, practically had to have a gun pointed at them to get them to spruce up.

The Chatter Box is a suitable name for a building that is shaped like a box and contains dozens of women whose favorite pastime, even when the window unit drowns them out, is chattering.

CHATTER BOX HAIR SALON
MEN & WOMEN 948-7505
OPEN

In this twenty-five-year-old shop, an empty pickle barrel holds beauty magazines, which contain hairdos customers can only dream about. Rachell Dowda does the latest cuts and the wash-and-sets with equal finesse. She's especially adept at twisting hair around the cigarette-sized rollers for a permanent wave.

Hair Barn

**DOUGLASVILLE
GEORGIA**

Hair-For-You

DOUGLASVILLE
GEORGIA

■ *Owner Donna Freeman prefers to watch her customers instead of the clock in the paneled shop where she's worked for about ten years. Time stops still when things are going well.*

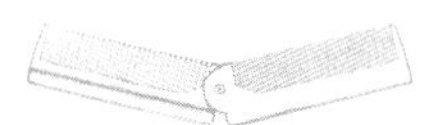

American Style
inspire
HERITAGE WEST
BEAUTÉ

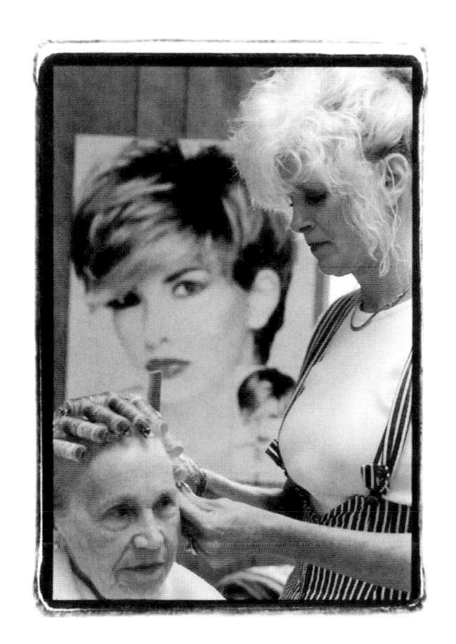

like silk
kerasilk
GOLDWELL Only at your hairdresser's

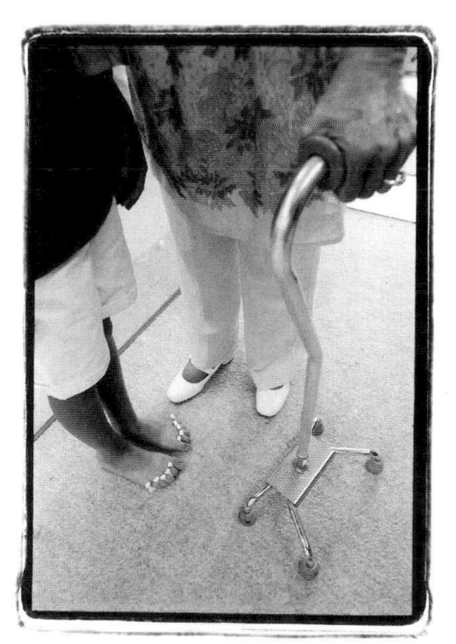

Fountain of Beauty

■

NEW ORLEANS
LOUISIANA

With his head thrown back and both hands waving in the air, Louis Truxillo pads across the wooden floor of his French Quarter salon like some kind of Baryshnikov of Beauty. His movements are graceful and fluid. His denim pants swish gently above his white leather loafers.

He answers the phone on his antique desk and informs the caller that cornrows are not a specialty of the Fountain of Beauty. Then he pads back to the red vinyl swivel chair where seventy-six-year-old Dot Truxillo (no relation to Louis) waits to have her platinum blond hair teased halfway to heaven.

In white pants, white sandals, and a canary yellow blouse, Mrs. Truxillo drove thirty minutes from Arabi, Louisiana, as she has once a week for the last ten years, to get her hair done by Louis. Like many of his clients, she's something of a high-society matron, an officer with one of the Mardi Gras carnival events, and she's convinced that of all the beauticians in Greater New Orleans, only Louis truly knows how to do her hair.

He couldn't agree more. "Dot tells me what to do, and I ignore her," the stylist says as he whips that white mane into a fluffy meringue while Fats Domino warbles "Blueberry Hill" over the salon sound system.

"I give her a big 'do, with a flip on the right side," Louis says. "She comes to me 'cause nobody else knows how to tease anymore. I have beauty students who want to pay me to come watch me tease. They don't teach that in beauty school. It's a dying art form."

"Next week," Mrs. Truxillo tells him, "I want you to put it in a twist." Then, as if Louis is no longer there, she confides, "He can do anything to anybody's hair. People ask me all the time where I get mine done."

By the time Mrs. Truxillo is ready to leave, her hair is so big she appears to be wearing a white sombrero that teeter-totters atop her head.

"Dot tells me what to do, and I ignore her," says Louis about one of his faithful customers.

Even after thirty years in the beauty business, Louis still loves the glamor-girl look. And lately, he says, the classy ladies are hard to find.

"All men like that look," Louis declares. "The masculine male, whether he's in France or China or Israel or the desert, likes a woman to look like a woman. That's the biggest mistake girls make—trying to be casual. They say they don't want to look like whores. Well most of 'em that don't want to look like a whore are whores. They just give it away. So they're not prostitutes."

Louis likes to talk, but there are a few things his customers and employees don't know about the raspy-voiced, brown-haired former military man. One is his age. Estimates range from fifty to seventy-five, depending on the person you ask and how mad at Louis that person may be at the moment. Two things everybody knows about this colorful New Orleans native are that he adores screen siren Betty Grable and he

has a tongue sharp enough to slice bread and then butter every piece.

Yet if a client should talk ugly, well that's another story. "I have thrown out that door and into the street a girl whose father was a very big politician because she used the F-word," Louis says, just minutes after using the word himself. "I threw her out in the street, and she cried for three months. Her father called and asked if I'd please take her back, and I said 'No.'

"The young girls come in now, and they use that word all the time. I use it, but my rule is nobody under thirty can use it. Whatever happened to class?

"A good hairdresser is like a doctor to a patient."

It's all trash now. You could ruin somebody's hair today, and they'd love it."

Louis, understandably, is often short of personnel. He relies on longtime friends like Laurie Mascair to assist him in the salon. "My job is, I take his abuse," says Laurie, a pretty, if unglamorous, thirty-four-year-old who has worked for Louis just three weeks and is already declaring her plans to quit.

"My dead mother used to come here to get her hair done," Laurie recalls. "She'd say to me, 'Put some makeup on, put some curlers in your hair, you'll find a man.' Louis tells me the same thing. 'You women in your T-shirts and jeans, you look like a man. In Paris, women wear dresses.' He loves to go to Paris. I just ignore him, like I did my mother."

The Fountain of Beauty, like its owner's tastes, harks back to the glamor days of the 1930s and '40s, when a proper woman would rather die than be seen on the street without makeup and a perfect coiffure. A faux-marble counter stretches across one mirrored wall illuminated by a row of globe lights. The nonstop music has switched from Fats Domino to big band. Rare movie posters of Miss Grable and other glamor girls of a bygone era line every wall.

There's a photo of Mae West, signed "*Sincerely.*" Louis's cast of pinups includes Alice Faye, Zsa Zsa Gabor, and Rita Hayworth. He owns a drinking glass that once touched the lips of Marilyn Monroe.

Sweet Rosie O'Grady, Diamond Horseshoe, The Dolly Sisters, Moon Over Miami—Louis not only has seen each of those Betty Grable movies several times

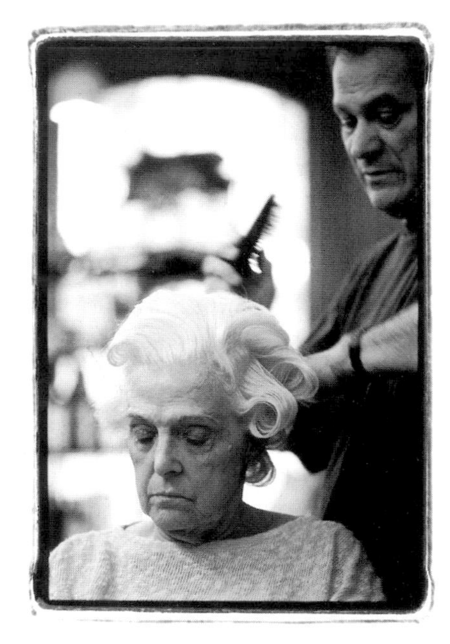

"She comes to me 'cause nobody else knows how to tease anymore," says Louis. "It's a dying art form."

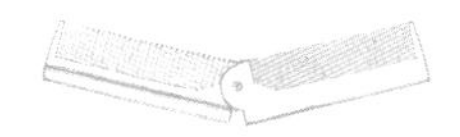

but can also name Miss Grable's costars and the year the film hit the big screen. "When I was young, all the kids went to the movies and collected movie-star stuff, and Betty Grable was my favorite of all," he says. "Every poster, scrapbook, every trinket that was ever put out with her picture on it, I've got it.

"The first time I met her was in 1969. I traveled to Las Vegas to see her. Everything I had been told or imagined, she was it. She was the most beautiful, the most talented, the most ladylike—not only to me. For ten years she was the number one actress in the world."

One of Louis's treasures is a full-length photograph of Miss Grable autographed by the star. "For Louis," she wrote. "Best wishes for the best of everything. Betty Grable."

Although he never got the chance to fix his idol's hair, Louis has coiffed many a celebrity who's come to New Orleans to make a movie or enjoy a holiday. He did a day's work on the movie *Cincinnati Kid,* styling the likes of Steve McQueen, Ann-Margret, and Tuesday Weld. "You see people in reality like that, then you see them in the movies, and you know what makeup can do," Louis says with characteristic tact.

More recently he did hair and makeup for the movie *Night of Blood Horror,* with Gerald McRaney, and he even took screen credit in lieu of his $2,000 fee. "I combed out Judy Garland when she was here on her honeymoon after her fourth marriage," he says. "I've done Lana Turner, Vivian Blaine, Sebastian Cabot, Margaret O'Brien. I met Alice Faye, but I didn't do her hair. Willie Nelson's been here, Annie Lennox—all the big stars. Everybody who's anybody comes here when they're in New Orleans.

"I get people from all over the world," Louis says. "The first thing they tell me is they can't find a shop unless it's in a mall with somebody who just started yesterday and doesn't know what a roller is. A good hairdresser is like a doctor to a patient. The more homely a person is, the more they're in need of going to a beauty shop. I tell them that.

"A lot of people come in and want something, and I say, 'It's not for you.' Because if they tell other people they got it here, my customers would stop coming. If they insist, I'll keep trying to talk them out of it. Most shops you go into, they're in it for the money. They'll put a chamber pot on your head and send you out the door telling you how good it looks."

In the heyday of Louis's shop, and of the glamorous Big Easy nightlife, Louis tended not only to the society women but also to the ladies of the evening, who often worked in the afternoons as well. "We'd open at nine in the morning and do all the grand old ladies of New Orleans, all the rich clientele of Uptown and the French Quarter, and at three o'clock all the strippers and whores would come in. Every day I was afraid one would run into the other. But as the last lady left, the first whore would come in. I did a lot of whores—professionals, prostitutes, singers, dancers, entertainers—until seven at night.

"Sometimes in the mornings, I'd have a judge's wife sitting next to a call girl, and nobody knew the difference. Because a call girl then was very, very fashionable. They weren't trashy-looking; they weren't gaudy. Some girls I did three times a day. They'd come in at nine in the morning, get a manicure and pedicure and shampoo-and-set, and then leave and have a date with a man at noon. They'd go to a hotel 'til one, and then they'd come and get a red wig for after lunch. After the second trick, usually some judge or politician or congressman, they'd come back at 4:30, and I made 'em a brunette. And I'd make them tell me all about their date. If they didn't, I'd make them look like crap.

"Most shops . . . are in it for the money. They'll put a chamber pot on your head . . . telling you how good it looks."

"Sometimes they'd volunteer the information, and I kept their confidence. Only once did something happen. I had this woman who was very, very social, a prominent woman in her thirties, and she came every Friday, and she'd tell me she had to be ready by one because she had to meet her cousin for lunch. After six months of this, her husband called one day right after she left. I said, 'She's gone—she had to meet her cousin.' And he said, 'She has no cousin by that name.' I said, 'Of course she does—they meet every Friday for lunch at this hotel.'

"Of course that caused a lot of trouble. She came in, and I said, 'You should have told me. Because the rest of these whores tell me what they're doing, and I tell their husbands they're shopping. Since you wanted to be so damn sneaky, you got caught.' "

In those days one of Louis's best customers was a French Quarter showgirl named Chris Owens, who is now a legendary Bourbon Street entertainer. "I swear she's a man," offers Laurie, Louis's assistant. "Louis says no. But she looks like a drag queen to me."

Through the years Louis's main competitor has been a soft-spoken, almost shy man named Ronald Leeke, who has run the city's oldest beauty shop, Salon de Belle Dame, on Dumaine Street, since 1959. The name is French for "beautiful lady." Leeke grew up in Laurel, Mississippi, and, like Louis, spent four years in the air force before going into the beauty business. Leeke is also a former dancer. His beauty license, posted on the wall, depicts him in a pose right out of *Saturday Night Fever.*

For all their similarities, Louis and Leeke are as different as a brunette and a blond. Asked about Louis, Leeke is silent, but his face assumes an expression that suggests he's just sniffed a pair of dirty socks.

Of Leeke, Louis says, "We're all enemies. Not really. If I fire somebody, he'll hire 'em five minutes later. When I opened this salon, he had a huge shop. Before I opened, I got my hair cut there. After that I've never been in another beauty shop. I don't want to know what they're doing."

When Louis was growing up in New Orleans, the last thing he was interested in was hair. After graduating from Nichols High School, he joined the air force for a four-year tour that took him to a U.S. air base in France, not far from Paris. Because he quickly learned to speak fluent French, the air force wives began coaxing him to go with them to the local beauty school and serve as translator when they got their hair done. Soon the French stylists were telling him he should be in the beauty business.

"A lady would say she wanted her hair short, and I'd say, 'No, no, no, no—you shouldn't do that.' Or if she wanted it blond, I'd say, 'No, no, no.' I have an eye for beauty and art. They said, 'You'd be great in the beauty business.' I said, 'No, I cannot stand to work around women. The last thing in the world I need is a bunch of women ordering me what to do.' "

After the service, when he got back to New Orleans, Louis found that his younger brother had enrolled in beauty school. Louis watched him work with their mother, learning how to apply bleach and rollers. But Louis kept his job with an insurance company until a few years later when his girlfriend needed some quick beautifying.

"One night she decided she was going out to this big party. I was home sick with the flu. Anyway she went to the party and came home about 11:30, and her hair was all messed up. She started changing clothes, saying she was going to a big formal dinner at

midnight. I said, 'How in the hell can you go lookin' like that? Look at your hair!' "

Louis fixed her some coffee and sat her down at the kitchen table. While she sipped, he took out all her hairpins and redid her upswept coiffure. Ten minutes later she took a cab to the party.

"A half hour goes by, and this girl calls and asks to speak to Chicky's boyfriend. I said, 'That's me.' She said, 'Can I come over for a comb-out? I'm going to a party.' I said, 'What the hell's a comb-out?' She said, 'Can you fix my hair?' I said, 'I don't know how to fix hair.' She said, 'Well you did Chicky's just fine.' I told her all I did was straighten it out. She said, 'I'll give you $50 if you'll straighten mine out.' I said, 'Get over here!' "

Within a couple of weeks, Louis was doing a thriving beauty business among Bourbon Street entertainers. In his spare time he took classes at American Beauty School, where, he says, he learned he had a talent that needed little nurturing. "The owner said to me, 'Louis, every once in a while, we have somebody like you, gifted and talented, and no lessons are going to change the talent you have.' I stayed there about six months, went to another beauty school for about three months, and then opened my shop on Chartres Street with ten employees."

The name Fountain of Beauty came from a dream Louis had about a salon "where women would sip champagne and get their hair done."

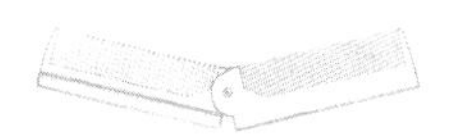

A year later he moved the business to Toulouse Street, where it's been ever since. The name Fountain of Beauty came from a dream he had, while he was still in beauty school, about a salon with a gorgeous fountain "where women would sip champagne and get their hair done."

In the early days the beehive was the rage, and Louis gave his an extra twist. "I'd do it high as it would go, and then I'd take my card and put it in the beehive hole. I did a wedding one time, with beehives and all, and I had my business cards sticking out of the holes. One of the girls in the wedding, the first one I finished, she paraded up to the corner to get some film. When she got back, she said, 'I need another card. The cashier wanted to know where I had my hair done, and she took the card.' "

And then there was the lady who visited once a week and invariably went to sleep under the dryer. "We'd turn out the lights and close the door and then knock and say, 'It's eight o'clock, is Louis open yet?' "

His storytelling is interrupted when an unlikely customer walks in—a tall, balding, recently retired New Orleans police lieutenant named Henry Aschebrock. "He had hair when he first started coming here," Louis says. "Now he comes in when I need the money."

The former cop remains nonplussed. "This is the place you want to be to find out everything you want to know," he says. Louis nods. "A lot of people have gotten their college degree right here," he says.

"I met Louis in my employment with the police," Aschebrock says, smiling at the sinister implication. "He came highly recommended for a number of things. This place is always full of characters."

"Liberace came in one time, and all the ladies went wild," Louis announces, the perfect non sequitur. "Turns out he just wanted the blue rinse."

As Frank Sinatra croons softly in the background, the stylist launches into another favorite tale—of the beautiful young brunette who walked in one day and asked Louis how much it would cost to make her a blond. When he told her it would take two days and $100, she asked if she could pay him a few dollars a day, on a kind of layaway plan.

"Every day she'd come in with $2, $5, $10, whatever she had, until she had paid it up. Then one Saturday morning around eleven, the busiest day of the week, she walked in, and the place was packed. We had every woman who was anybody in New Orleans. You could drop their first names, and the whole city would know who you were talking about. So she walks in, and I say, 'Listen, go to the back and put on a smock, and I'm gonna get my assistant to start working on you.' So she went in the back, went in the dressing room, and came out stark naked and walked all the way to the front of the shop. Not a word was said by anybody. Finally she says, 'I'm ready, but I couldn't find a smock.'

"I made her get back in there and put some clothes on. She said, 'You've got to forgive me. I'm so used to posing for the artists and dancing nude.' She ran in the back, put on a smock, and nobody said a word.

"That's what it's like working in the French Quarter. In this business I'd have been bored to death after three months if I were out of the Quarter. My brother has a neighborhood shop where every person is a repeat of the week before. A stranger never walks in.

"In this salon I've got women who've been coming here every week for thirty years, and every week they leave here a little bit different. They're never done the same. I create as I go along. Some of these older women go to salons, and it's like a puzzle they put together every week to make them look like 1961 or 1981. I can't do that. If I do a flip on a lady, every week it's different."

Louis, a bachelor, has done well for himself. He travels often to Paris. Besides his home in Slidell, he keeps an apartment above his salon, which isn't quite as busy as it used to be. The big-name strippers are mostly gone now. The hookers, he says, aren't elegant any more.

And there's that general disappearance of glamor among the masses that once celebrated big hair and pancake makeup. But the natural look is clearly not for Louis. "Years ago a lot of the restaurants wouldn't let these girls in unless they were in formal ball gowns. Now jeans and sweats are acceptable.

"I've got women who've been coming here every week for thirty years, and every week they leave here a little bit different."

"New Orleans is still the number one city in sales of formal gowns because of the Mardi Gras season. December 29th you have your first ball gown, and then the next night you don't want to repeat the dress, so you have to buy another.

"When I first came here, we'd do these fabulous hairdos. Now you can't get a girl to go out on the street with hair like that. The women are dressing more like men every day. They're getting their hair cut more like men every day. Unless there's a great turnaround in fashion, I don't know what it's going to be like ten years from now."

Louis sighs, a faraway look in his eyes. Then it's time for a revelation. "I could never be a woman," he says. "I couldn't go through all that makeup and crap." ■

In the land of Mardi Gras, a lot of attention is paid to hair. Because with all those banquets and balls to attend, a Louisiana lady must have a well of beauty she knows won't run dry, unlike those crude oil gushers off-shore in the Gulf. Perhaps the most ethnically mixed of all the Southern states, Louisiana produces some of your more exotic hairdos as well, often concocted by intriguing characters with dark complexions and thick Cajun accents. In New Orleans in particular, there's a tendency for beauticians to promote bigger as better and platinum blond as perfection in a peroxide bottle. So it isn't just the strippers who wander the French Quarter balancing tall, yellow artworks on top of their heads. As one beautician declared, "Women's looks have gone to hell. We need more damn glamor in the world."

Lords & Ladies

PONCHATOULA
LOUISIANA

To keep out the riffraff, or perhaps just because it sounds so classy, this salon calls itself Lords & Ladies. But it's just a fancy way of saying Men & Women, which a sign inside takes pains to explain. The Ladies, by the way, out-number the Lords, probably because the Lords aren't as inclined to suffer the indignities of the permanent wave.

Sometimes things get so busy at Lords & Ladies that the customers seem to come and go in a dizzying blur. Then again, sometimes the business is like a Sunday afternoon—slow, easy, and downright relaxing. For many customers, it's their only chance to sit back with a newspaper, particularly one of those grocery-store tabloids that most wouldn't be caught dead reading outside the beauty parlor.

Salon de Belle Dame

NEW ORLEANS
LOUISIANA

At Salon de Belle Dame in New Orleans' French Quarter, wilted tourists often stop by for a fluff-up, performed by the shop's longtime male owner, who also happens to be a former dancer. But hair's not the only thing he knows how to fix. If your nails, like your coiffure, need a touch of color, then sit in the chair and put up your feet.

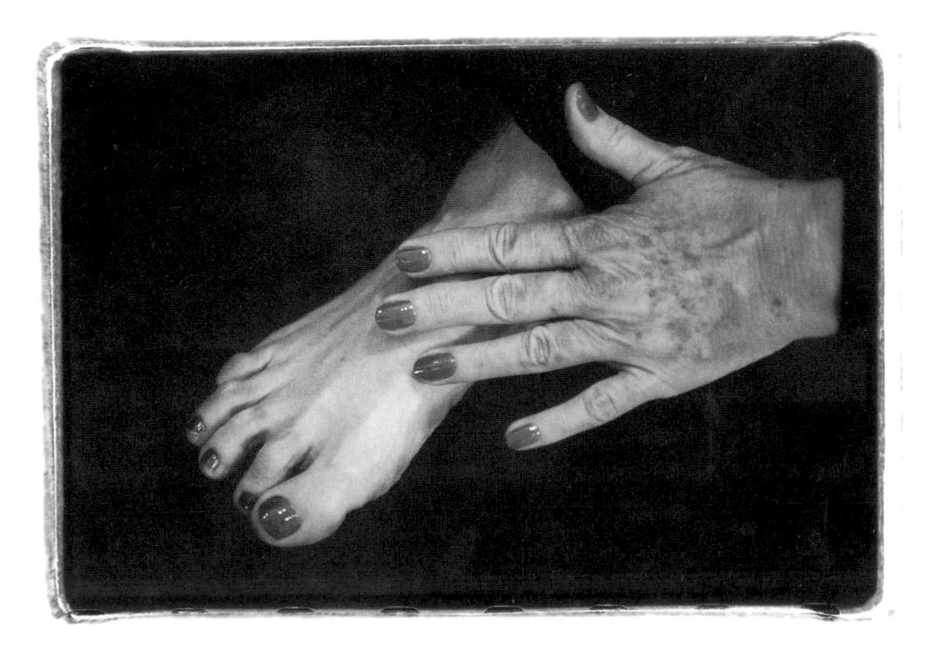

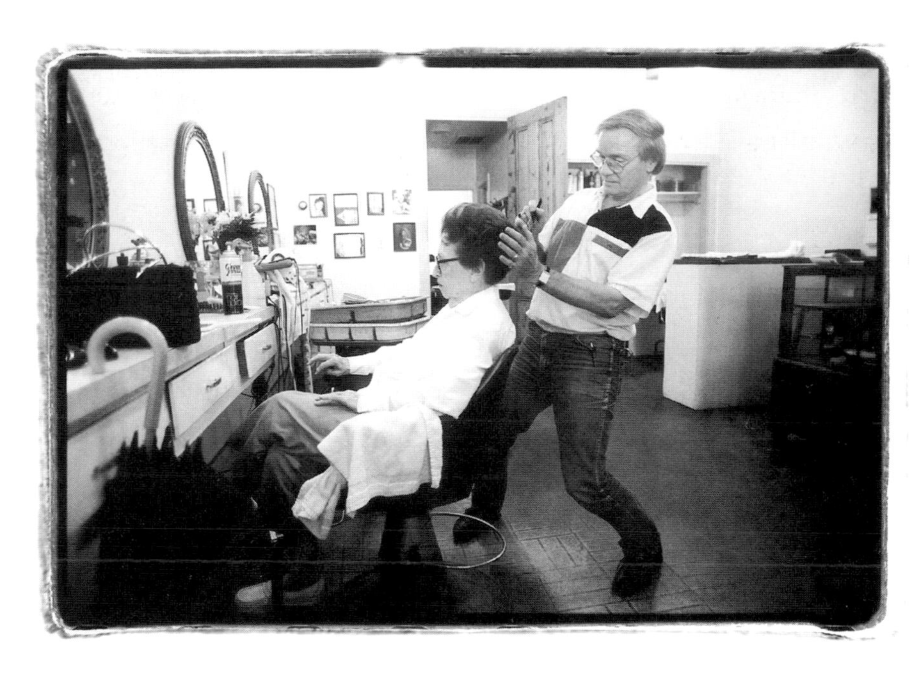

R. Leeke
527 Dumaine St.
New Orleans, LA 70116

SIGNATURE

EGISTRATION

Louisiana State Board of Cosmetology
INDUSTRIPLEX
11622 SUNBELT COURT
BATON ROUGE, LA 70809

EDWIN W. EDWARDS
GOVERNOR
JOEL C. MUMPHREY
CHAIRMAN
FRAN CALVET
VICE CHAIRMAN

LICENSE

TYPE Cosmetologist
DATE 08/22/1995
FEE $15.00

THIS IS TO CERTIFY THAT

Ronald C. Leeke
527 Dumaine St.
New Orleans LA 70116

CERTIFICATE OF REGISTRATION

th the Louisiana Laws pertaining to Cosmetic Therapy and has
ertificate is not transferrable.

Peeking inside Salon de Belle Dame from the sidewalk on Dumaine Street, window-shoppers get an intriguing glimpse of this old-fashioned house-of-beauty. When business is slow, which it often is, owner Ronald Leeke reads the newspaper and listens to talk radio. But the one-time dancer, who posed like a Rockette for his cosmetology license, is quick on his feet when a lady is in his chair.

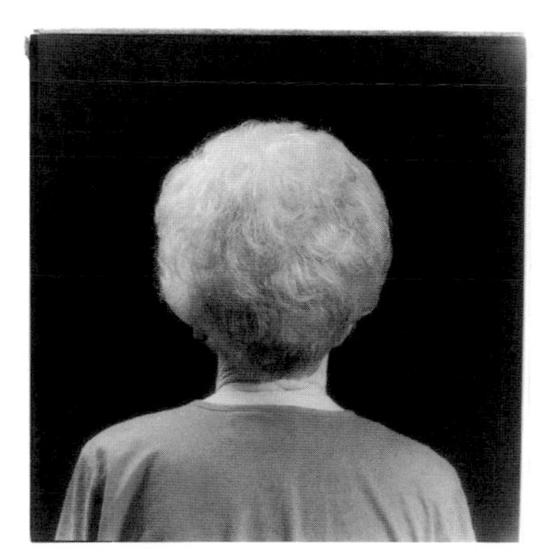

Headquarters Style Shop

■

MERIDIAN
MISSISSIPPI

It's a Saturday afternoon in early February, but inside the Headquarters Style Shop in downtown Meridian, Mississippi, the Christmas tree has yet to come down. While the festive fake fir is the predominant decoration, it competes for attention with an assortment of wooden rabbits (commemorating Easter); red, white, and blue streamers (for the Fourth of July); heart-shaped boxes (for Valentine's Day); and a horn of plenty (Thanksgiving will be here before you know it).

"We have a decoration up for every holiday of the year," declares beautician Teresa Long, the owner of the oldest barber and beauty shop in this east Mississippi city. "In here, we're celebrating all the time."

Longtime customer Peggy Griffith, who's getting her hair rolled two chairs away, feels the need to clarify. "They're just like me," Mrs. Griffith says of Teresa and her co-beautician, Sue Martin. "They're just too sorry to take the stuff down."

Sue and Teresa agree and practically drop to the floor with laughter. Mrs. Griffith offers each woman another one of her homemade pralines. She brought the stuff in honor of Mardi Gras, which is going on a few hours down Interstate 59 in New Orleans. "I make them suckers," Mrs. Griffith declares as she dispenses a praline to a fellow customer. "A friend I went to school with, her Cajun friend gave her the recipe. Aren't they the best things you ever tasted?"

All the ladies ooh and aah and generally agree that their taste buds will never be the same. "Does anybody know how Mardi Gras got started?" asks Teresa as she trims the curly red hair of Jo Graham, who's fifty-seven and works in insurance. "I think it's religious," Sue says. Teresa looks confused. "I thought it was when we got our emancipation from France," she says. Sue shakes her head and states with authority, "It was definitely religious."

Mrs. Griffith provides the usual analysis: "Some lyin' gets done in here."

Ms. Graham interrupts the nonstop dialogue to tell Teresa she likes her "tags," the wispy curls that glide down the back of Ms. Graham's head. "I told her they'd make her young and sexy," Teresa says. Offers Sue, "And them's the right words for our little customers."

"Some lyin' gets done in here," says Mrs. Griffith.

Part of the pleasure of doin' hair, Teresa says, is interviewing the customers. "I usually talk to Jo about her love life, her diet, all the gossip. I'm the gossiper here. I pray for myself. I'm trying to watch that. But Meridian is such a small town, less than 50,000, and we gossip if somebody buys a new pair of shoes." Sue hollers her agreement: "We talk about how much they cost."

As Sue rolls Mrs. Griffith's dark hair, the customer watches Sue's every move

in the wall-length mirror. A cattle farmer, Mrs. Griffith, sixty-two, has come here for a decade, ever since Teresa bought the old Watkins Barber Shop and turned it into a house-of-beauty.

Long before Sue settled down for business at one of the three chairs facing the long mirror, she was Mrs. Griffith's favorite beautician. Their relationship dates back to 1976, when Sue worked in another salon and Mrs. Griffith auditioned her for her weekly wash-and-set.

"Can't you tell how beautiful I am?" Mrs. Griffith asks, eyeing her curled-up locks in the mirror. "That's why I keep coming. I've been following Sue all over town for twenty years. I think we started there at Michaeline's, right up the street. Then we went to Guys and Dolls, then Patsy's, then Helen's, and then here. We talk about our children, and recipes, and my cows, and her daddy's cows, and my friends, and her friends, and their cows. We just never shut up.

"I just like the way Sue does my hair," Mrs. Griffith continues. "If I'm late, that's fine. If she's late, that's fine. I like her as a friend. I have to like someone to sit with 'em two hours. Sometimes it takes even longer to make me beautiful."

A grinning Teresa glances at Mrs. Griffith, who's gotten herself so tickled she can barely talk. "Look how good she looks at sixty-two," Teresa says as Sue's customer goes into a spasm of giggles. "Actually, we don't have no ugly customers. If they are ugly, they're not when they get out of here. We don't have any mean ones either."

Teresa and Sue work just a dozen feet apart. Teresa has the chair by the window, and Sue the chair by the wall. In the middle is the third chair, which periodically gets occupied by a third beautician, though usually not for long.

"Through the years, I think we've had six other people in that middle chair," Teresa says. "If Sue likes 'em, they stay a while. If not, they're out the door. Sue doesn't like 'em if they try to steal her customers, especially the men customers."

Because Headquarters was a barber shop for more than half a century, the beauticians count among their clientele a small number of men. Male lawyers from the county courthouse across the street regularly stop by for a trim. "We hear all about their cases, especially the ones involving prostitution and gambling," Teresa says. She tends to most of the men and to the women who prefer a cut-and-blow dry. The weekly wash-and-curls are Sue's specialty.

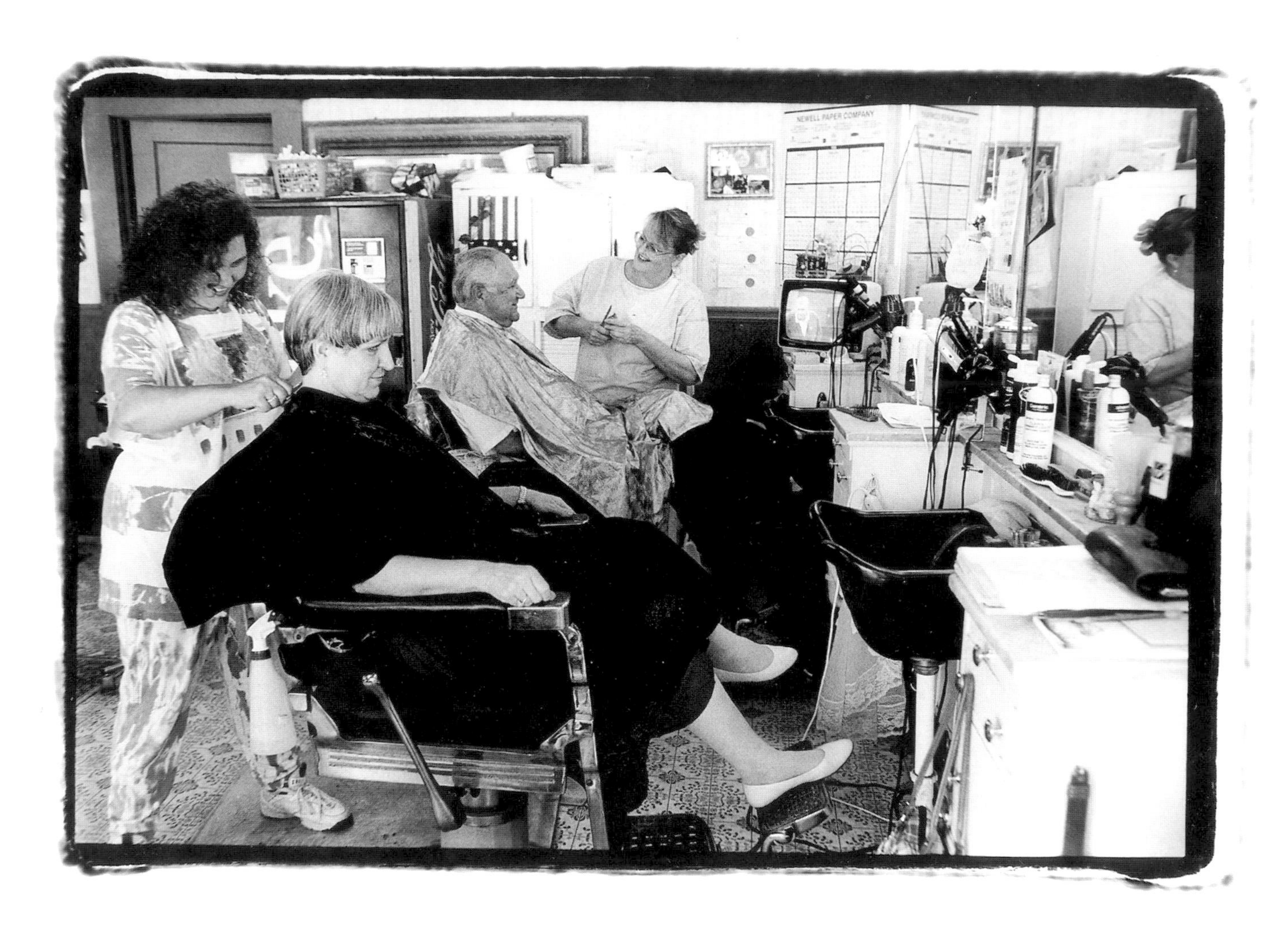

"There's older beauticians in town, but I don't think there's a shop older than this," Teresa says. Most of the fixtures are original, including the three chrome-trimmed, ox-blood leather barber chairs (one even has an attached strap for sharpening razors), the long mirror, the ceramic sinks, the yellowing marble counter, and the linoleum floor.

When Teresa first visited the old barber shop, in the ninety-year-old yellow-brick Dement Printing Co. building, she wasn't thinking about buying it. Rather, she wanted to purchase the antique barber chairs that, along with the shop, were for sale. "I bought the chairs and decided to stay. We've tried to keep it real authentic," Teresa says as a fan whirs from the center of the 15-foot-high ceiling.

Although she has an accent straight out of *Steel Magnolias,* Teresa has ventured far beyond the moss-draped mysteries of Mississippi. Her father, Fred Wedgeworth, was a career air force officer, and he moved around the country with his wife, Mattie, and five children, Teresa being the youngest.

"He needs a haircut," the mother of a four-year-old says, as if Teresa might prefer to give him a permanent wave and a manicure.

"When my father went to Vietnam in 1968, my mother and I came here," she says. "Mother was originally from here but had been away about forty years." Although Teresa was barely a teenager then, it didn't take her long to grow up. By the time she graduated from Meridian's Southeast High School in 1976, she had married, given birth to a daughter, and gotten a divorce. "I'm on my third husband now. My first marriage lasted only a year. He had a really neat car, one of those Chargers, hot pink and all. It was sharp."

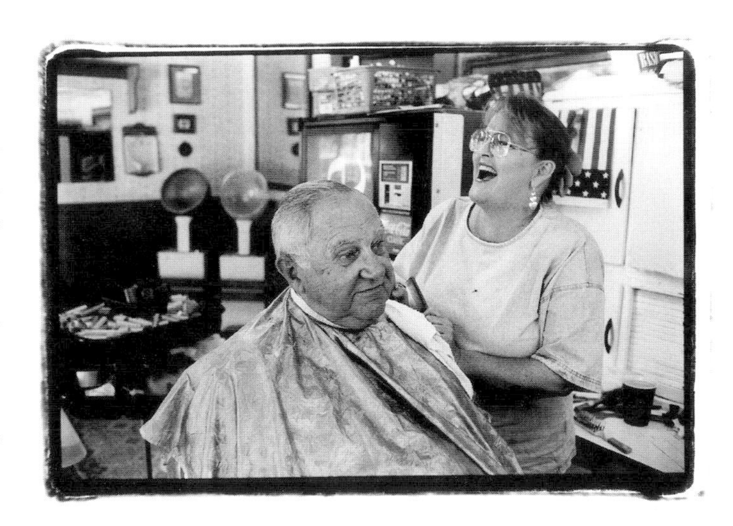

In the midst of this story, a female customer walks in and deposits her four-year-old son in Teresa's chair. "He needs a haircut," the mother says, as if Teresa might prefer to give him a permanent wave and a manicure. About the time Teresa is ready to pick up her tale, the fluorescent lights go out. The silence of the hair dryers causes sleeping customers to suddenly wake up.

"This happens all the time," Teresa says as she goes to the breaker box and mashes a button, reviving the beauty parlor's buzz and lights. "The wiring's old and we're always blowing a fuse. We might have to get that fixed one day."

All trimmed up, the little boy looks down from the barber chair, points to the floor, and says to his mother, "Those my hairs!" Teresa asks him if he gets his good looks from his mom or dad. "Dad," the child says, watching his mother's face in the mirror.

Years ago Teresa studied art for a time at Ole Miss and even thought about becoming an art teacher. It was during those days in Oxford that she first worked in a beauty parlor. It was a way to put her art training to use without having to suffer too many little boys and other classroom miseries. She worked in a string of other salons before opening Headquarters in 1986. She figures she averages thirteen customers a day.

Tonight she and a dozen girlfriends, including Sue, will dine in a casino in nearby Philadelphia to celebrate Teresa's upcoming thirty-ninth birthday. "I'm actually going to be thirty-nine, not like all these women that claim to be," she says. "Of course, I don't know how many years I'm going to stay thirty-nine."

Throughout the afternoon, Teresa fields phone calls from friends wanting to know what she's wearing to the celebration. With the telephone cradled against her ear, she waves at Beverly Rhodes, who arrives for a haircut. "I'm wearing a long dress, but it's still casual," the beautician says into the phone.

"She's such a good operator, real pleasant and all."

Meanwhile Sue combs out and shellacs Dot Espey, who comes in every Saturday at noon, along with her ninety-one-year-old mother, Annie Boswell, to get their near-identical gray hair beautified by Sue. Mrs. Espey, sixty-seven, who works as an insurance supervisor at a local hospital, says nobody can do her hair like Sue.

"She's such a good operator, real pleasant and all," says Mrs. Espey, a fashion plate in a crisp red blazer, red sweater, and black wool pants. Her mother, looking equally stylish in purple pants and a white sweater, smiles and nods. "We haven't run Mother off yet with all we talk about," Teresa says, smiling at the older woman. Mrs. Espey points out a mitigating factor: "You forget Mama's hard of hearing."

After Mrs. Espey pays for Sue's services, the beautician hugs both mother and daughter and tells them, "I love you."

Like most of her customers, Sue grew up in Meridian and, according to Teresa, who's too young to know for sure, was something of a flower child in the late 1960s. "She had a Volkswagen covered in flowers," Teresa says. Sue sets her straight: "It was a Corvair." "Anyway," Teresa says, "she was real cool."

Sue remembers when boys drove Corvettes, girls wore beehives, and everybody was crazy about Elvis. One time Sue even snuck her Super 8 movie camera into a Jackson concert hall and came away with some rare footage of The King in concert.

Sue spent her entire life in Meridian, except for a short stint in Pensacola, Florida, to attend beauty school. She was finishing her studies there in 1969 when one of the deadliest hurricanes of the century, Camille, blasted through. Sue remembers the devastation, especially along the Mississippi Gulf Coast, where for months after the killer storm, clothes hung in trees, boats lay on the beaches, and old plantations were piled in rubble for several blocks inland.

Sue decided to go directly to beauty school after graduating from West Lauderdale High School in 1968. "I've always liked doing hair. I didn't really have an ambition to go to college. A friend of my mother's was a beautician, and she kind of talked me into it. Mrs. Griffith says I did it 'cause I like to pull people's hair. That's probably it. Plus nowadays, you can't make nothin' goin' to college."

After returning to Meridian in late '69, Sue began working in a string of beauty parlors. A short marriage produced a daughter, who, at twenty-three, is the same age as Teresa's daughter. The two young women are good friends. Sue spends her free time going on cruises and traveling to far-off places, often in the company of one or more of her customers.

"This is my special comb," Sue announces when it's time to comb out Mrs. Griffith. She holds a blue piece of plastic that's missing most of its teeth. "Teresa threw it away, and I fished it out of the garbage," Sue says with pride. "I hold it so tight, I break the teeth right out of it."

Sue is big on teasing and spraying, which is what her once-a-week ladies need to keep them looking beautiful for seven days. "I send 'em home today, and they come back looking exactly the same, not a hair out of place," she brags.

Neither rain, sleet, nor severe weather can keep Sue from serving her customers. "One day we had this hurricane, and Teresa and her customers ran for cover in the courthouse, and I had to stay here," Sue reports. "My customer wouldn't leave with her hair all teased up."

Another terrifying episode occurred on a Wednesday night when Sue was combing out one of her wealthier ladies, who wore diamonds on nearly every finger. The two women were alone in the shop when all of a sudden, as Sue recollects, "Sirens came from every direction, and guys with spotlights and machine guns." A prisoner had escaped from the jail atop the courthouse, and Sue's customer was sure he was after her jewels. "I said, 'We can't leave, and we can't stay. What're we gonna do?' " Sue recalls. "My customer went in the bathroom and called her husband, like that was gonna help. Anyway, they eventually caught the guy before he got her diamonds."

Pushing a wisp of blond hair back toward her short ponytail, Sue frees Mrs. Griffith from under the dryer and adds a few minutes to another lady's drying time. "I have a lady that goes to sleep under

there, and if I'm busy, I'll go over and put some more time on her, and she comes out looking like that," Sue says, pointing to a newspaper cartoon taped to the mirror.

It depicts a shrunken-headed woman with smoldering rollers in her hair. Someone has written "Sue" over the hairdresser and "Arlene" over the woman with the shrunken head. ("We got Arlenes, Earlines, Paulines, and pralines," Sue says.)

According to Mrs. Griffith, Sue is forever telling Arlene that she'll be dry in "two more minutes, two more minutes. Of course, she's already been under there a couple of hours."

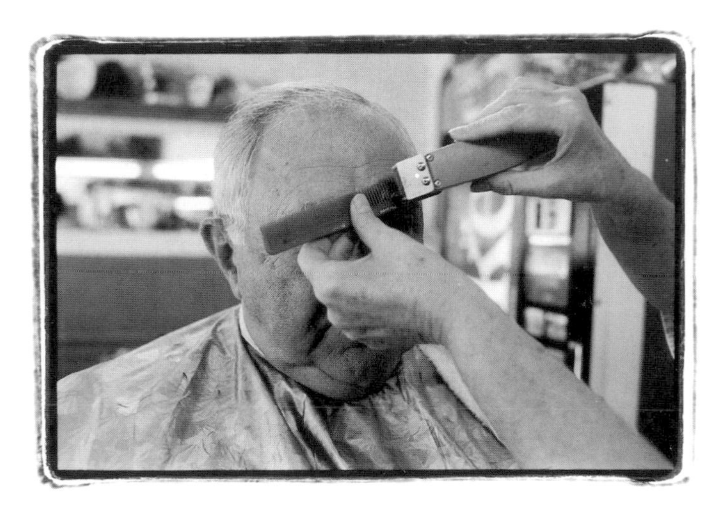

From across the shop, Teresa screams, "Look out! Look out! Look out!" as the brass coat tree by the door starts to topple, threatening the hairdo of a departing customer. The phone rings, Sue answers and talks for a minute, then hangs up and announces, "Alicia needs a frosting. She's desperate."

Teresa, meanwhile, greets customer Ken Covington, forty-four, a Meridian paper products salesman who also happens to be her old boyfriend. The two dated in 1986, before he married his wife, Lisa, and Teresa got hitched to her third husband, Brian, a fireman, who is the father of her four-year-old son.

"Ken's one of our all-time sports heroes," Teresa says, while Covington blushes under his "businessman's layered haircut," as Teresa calls it. "In high school, he played basketball, football, baseball, every kind of ball," she says. "I used to cut his hair. I cut everything he had."

"Ken's one of our all-time sports heroes," says Teresa. "I used to cut his hair. I cut everything he had."

Covington interjects weakly, "She didn't cut me for a while after we broke up." Once they mended the friendship, however, he was back in her chair, usually surrounded by women. "I don't think the ladies pay much attention to me," he says. Teresa disagrees. "You're lyin'. We put on our lipstick when we see you comin'."

As the afternoon winds down, Teresa and Sue are no less animated. Sue talks about her trips. Teresa tells customers about the progress of her new house, which is going up in a Meridian subdivision. And she repeats, for a new audience, her favorite beauty-shop stories.

"I hear about the affairs that go on in town. One time I had a lady sittin' in my chair, and another girl come up and heard her saying, 'So-and-so finally caught her husband. And she's got pictures to prove it.' After my customer left, the girl told me she was the one in the pictures."

Because her shop is downtown in an area frequented by homeless gentlemen who drink too much, Teresa no longer offers her male customers a shave. "You do it for one, you got to do it for 'em all, and I ain't about to shave these bums," Teresa says.

Occasionally one of the men will stop by anyway, which typically causes a stir. "I had a drunk guy come in and pass out in front of the door, and we had all these lovely ladies and children in here," Teresa says. "I called the police, and this officer comes in, steps over the drunk guy, and, I swear, says to me, 'So who's giving you the problem?' "

The shop door opens and in walks Teresa's aunt, Mary Evelyn Rutherford, a sixty-three-year-old preacher's wife who's blessed with one blue eye and one brown. She also has the gift of gab, which she doesn't hesitate to unwrap.

"You know how many famous people come from Mississippi?" Mrs. Rutherford asks as she settles down in Sue's chair. She doesn't wait for an answer. "Stella Stevens, William Faulkner, Tennessee Williams, and of course Elvis. People say Mississippi's a backwards place, but we've got all these talented people."

Before anybody can dispute that, Mrs. Rutherford reveals that her maiden name is Dollar, to the delight of her husband, who is fond of saying, "I'll always have a Dollar." How he gets a word in, we'll never know. "I met a nudist in that CPR course, and he told me how he had a motorcycle wreck and nobody stopped to help him," Mrs. Rutherford says.

"Next time we were on the road, we saw a motorcycle wreck, and this man bleeding from the head, and I said, 'Stop! That nudist had another wreck!' It turns out the man (who was not the nudist) had escaped from a New Orleans mental hospital. He had shippafrenia, or something like that."

With Mrs. Rutherford finally under a dryer, the beauticians stop for a cold drink. Soon they'll tackle a late-afternoon horde of adolescent girls in need of big hairdos for a local beauty pageant.

Sue sits in her chair and eats a praline. Teresa gets a Coke from the machine. She glances about the beauty shop.

"If these walls could talk, I bet they could tell you something about Meridian," she says dreamily. "All those old men that would come in here, the language probably wouldn't be fit to hear." Sue nods. Teresa takes a sip of her drink. "But I'd like to hear it anyway." ■

the state that gave us Elvis Presley has, like the King, a style all its own. What with the statewide influx of casino gambling, its nightlife is of a quality now greater than that of neighboring Alabama, which generally finishes 49th to Mississippi's No. 50 on most official ratings lists. Along with that nightlife, of course, comes a higher demand for feminine beauty, which can be acquired in places like C.J.'s Hair Fashions in Meridian. There a customer's grandson can get himself a Pepsi from the drink machine and enjoy a snack while Granny gets ready for a night at the slot machines.

C.J.'s Hair Fashions

MERIDIAN
MISSISSIPPI

Inside C.J.'s customers relax (and go under the dryer) in a living-room atmosphere, complete with television, magazines, and toys for the young'uns.

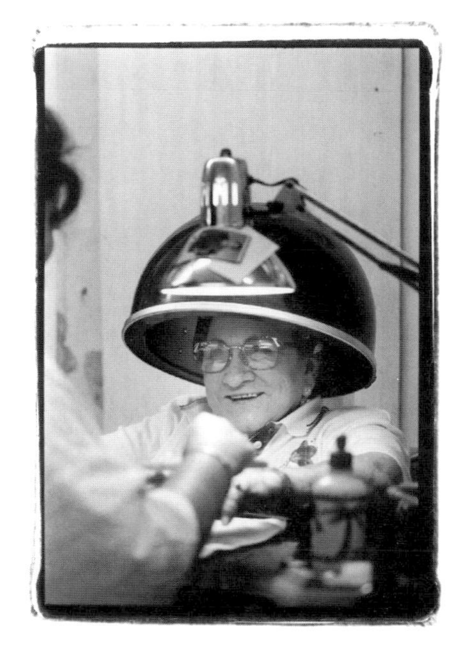

Creative Concepts Beauty Salon

BRANDON
MISSISSIPPI

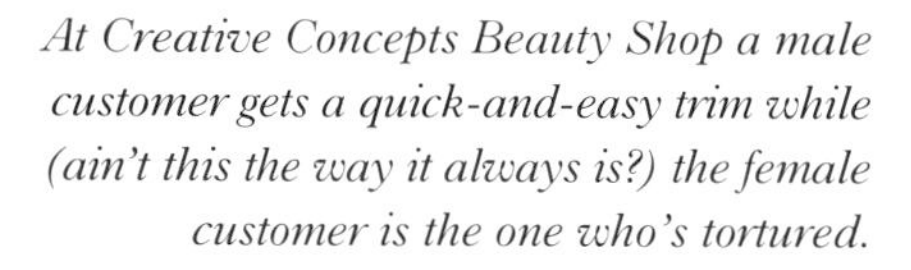

At Creative Concepts Beauty Shop a male customer gets a quick-and-easy trim while (ain't this the way it always is?) the female customer is the one who's tortured.

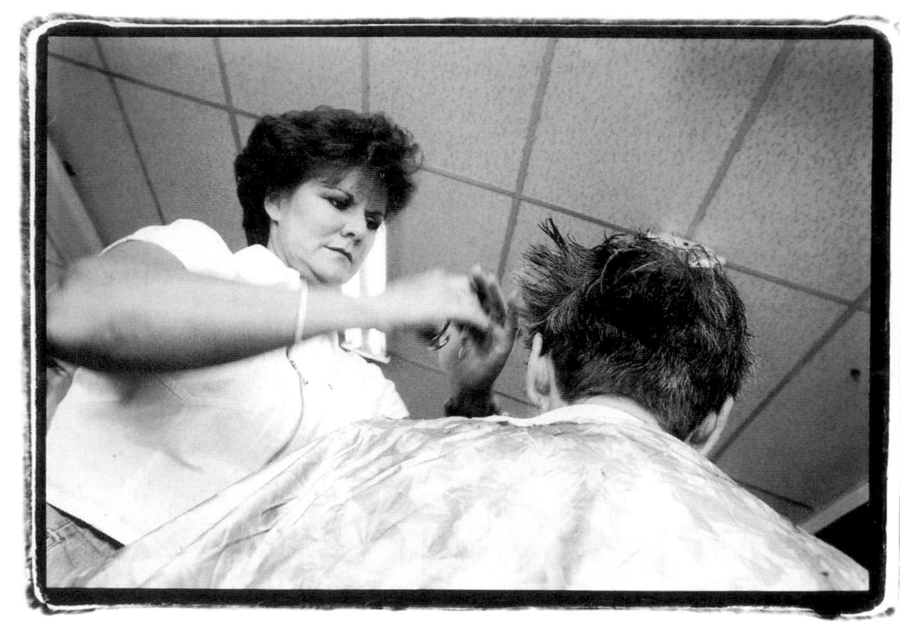

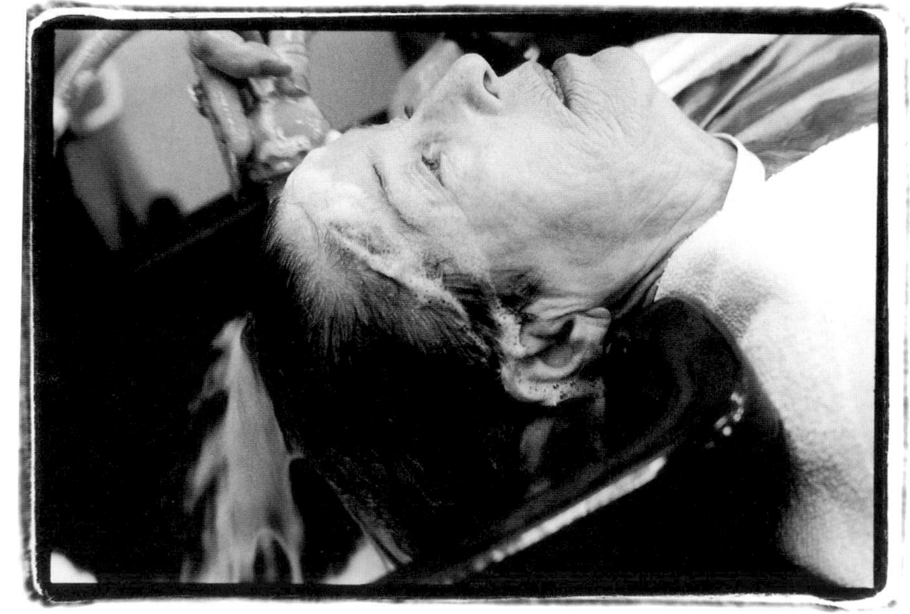

Sometimes it's just a woman and her operator, alone in a beauty shop on a Saturday afternoon, reflecting on the activities of the past week. When it comes down to it, many ladies like their beauticians more than they do certain family members.

Town West Hair Salon

BRANDON MISSISSIPPI

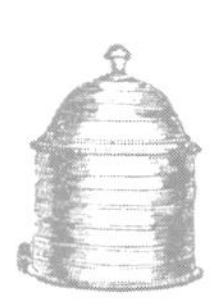

While the dryer heats her scalp, a customer in Town West Hair Salon reads a novel, fittingly titled "Caught in a Firestorm." On a nearby shelf, a faceless, bodiless mannequin models what looks like a bad toupee.

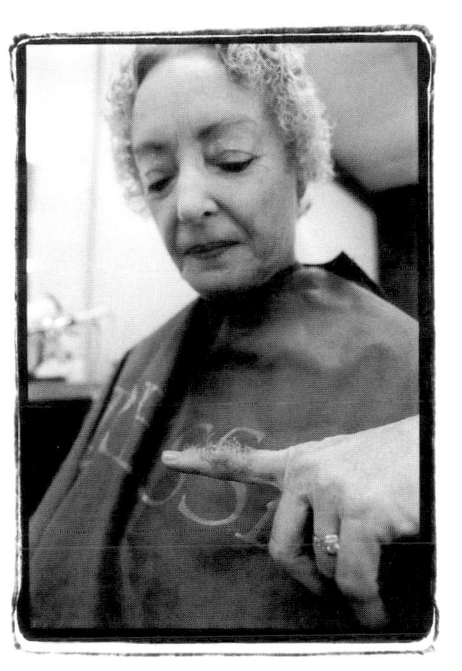

Inside Town West Hair Salon a finicky lady checks to see that the operator doesn't lop off too many of her curls. After her trim, she'll join a fellow customer for a Coke and a nap under the dryer.

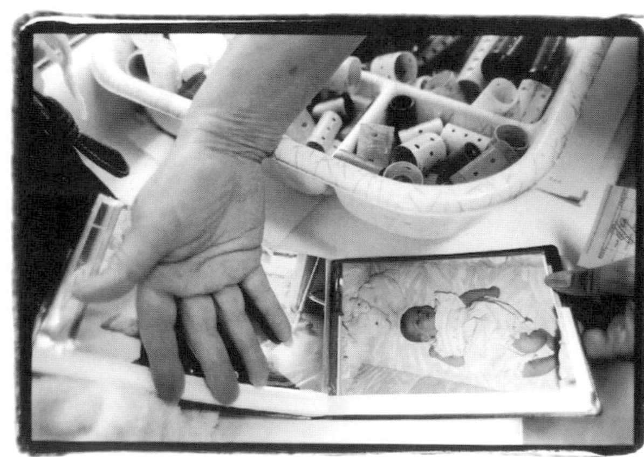

Shampoo + Set
$8.50

THANK YOU
WE'RE HAPPY FOR CUSTOMERS LIKE YOU

Brandon skier ranks among the state's best
BLAINE ALLEN
Scruggs — Womack
Aprille Renee Allen to marry Toby G. Andrews

Horse Shoe Hair Designs

■

HORSE SHOE
NORTH CAROLINA

Inside a baby-blue cinder-block building that sits between a tomato patch and the Southern Railroad tracks, a woman in white slacks and a flowery blouse is showing off her son's wedding pictures. "They had it in Long Island," explains Helen Tully, whose nasal narrative gives away the fact that she lived in New York herself before moving to the South a dozen years ago.

"Isn't the bride lovely," drawls Lucille Heffner, seventy-eight, as she prepares to go under the dryer. Dolores Kowalski, another transplanted Yankee, strolls over to look at the blue photo album propped on Mrs. Tully's lap. Sharing the spotlight with the wedding party is an Elvis impersonator, complete with white spangled jumpsuit and red satin cape. Mrs. Kowalski oohs and aahs over this.

"My son still thinks he's a teenager," Mrs. Tully complains, examining a photo of a smiling, bald, gray-bearded man standing next to a Michelle Pfeiffer look-alike in a white wedding dress.

"He was married to my darling daughter-in-law for twenty-six years, and then he went off the wall," Mrs. Tully continues. "We never had any inkling anything was wrong. My husband and I almost died when he bought that motorcycle. Then he started dating all these young chicks. He's fifty-two, and his new wife is twenty-nine. She used to work in Manhattan, in the tanning salons. He's been a good son. You can't live their lives for them. You just do the best you can."

Mrs. Tully announces that her son, a retired Long Island police detective who now restores antique cars, had a transvestite singer at his wedding. "My husband said to me, 'Isn't she beautiful?' and I said to him, 'I bet it's a man.'"

Beautician Frankie Rice, who's been listening to Mrs. Tully from across the room, interrupts to tell Mrs. Heffner to get herself under the dryer. Mrs. Heffner settles down on old "Betsy," the nickname Frankie and her sister have for that black vinyl dryer chair. "Take you a nap, Lucille," Frankie tells Mrs. Heffner. "I'll wake you up when it's over."

Although Mrs. Heffner can't hear a thing but the roar of the dryer, Mrs. Tully isn't about to stop talking. "Next week I'll show you my daughter's wedding pictures," she tells beautician Judy Coggins, who is Frankie's sister and the owner of Horse Shoe Hair Designs, in what used to be a paving company garage. An ancient green gas pump still stands in front of the beauty shop, a relic of days gone by.

Judy, forty-nine, and Frankie, forty-three, have run Horse Shoe Hair Designs for sixteen years in this tiny mill town on the edge of Pisgah National Forest near the Tennessee border. A little farther west loom the Great Smoky Mountains. "We have a lot of tourists around here," Frankie declares. "Lots of

"Take you a nap, Lucille," Frankie tells Mrs. Heffner. "I'll wake you up when it's over."

Northern people are moving in. They retire and like the weather here. We don't have the snow they get up there."

Frankie and Judy grew up in nearby Brevard, North Carolina, a cotton mill town, where their daddy, Frank Cairnes, was a carpenter, and their mother, Dissie, was a maid at the local college and full-time mama to the two girls and their younger brother. Although she never went to beauty school, Mrs. Cairnes showed a knack for hair.

"Every Saturday, all the mill wives would come to my mama's house to have her bobby-pin their hair," Frankie says. "She just had a talent. She never got paid for it. Nobody had any money to pay anything."

Watching their mother work her magic with those bobby pins intrigued the Cairnes girls, who soon began experimenting with each other's hair. "I remember Judy always fixing her hair before going to school, and when she'd get home, I'd have mine all rolled up to show her how good I could do, and it'd be sticking out everywhere, just terrible, and she'd tell me I did real good," Frankie says. "It wasn't 'cause she didn't want to hurt my feelings. She didn't have time to fool with me."

"I didn't know how to fix it," Judy says to Frankie, who breaks into the kind of uproarious laugh that gives everyone who hears it a case of the giggles.

"We did our mother's hair, anybody that would let us," Frankie says. "Our uncle came by drunk one night and passed out on the couch, and we peroxided him. He had to wear a cap 'til it grew back out." She laughs again.

As teenagers the girls enjoyed roller skating and beer drinking, Frankie says. "It was kind of boring around here. You had to make your own excitement." Although she's the younger sister, Frankie was the first to go to beauty school. After graduating from high school in 1971, she got married, had a baby, and then, at age twenty, enrolled at American Academy of Hair Styling in nearby Gastonia. But having three more babies in the next seven years temporarily

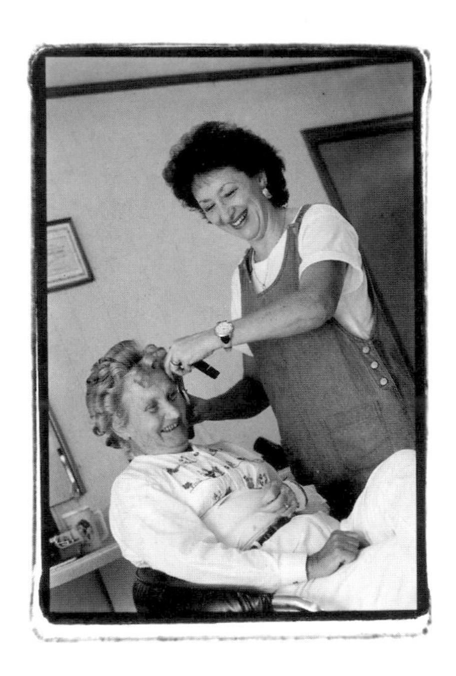

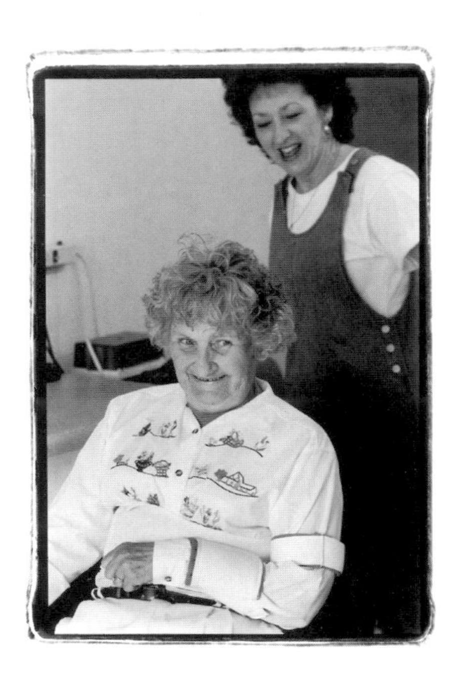

prevented her from going into the beauty business.

Judy, meanwhile, was also married and raising three children. When the last one was in school, she went to Western Carolina School of Cosmetic Arts in Hendersonville. "I enjoyed doing hair," Judy says. "And it was a short course, so I could finish in about a year and then have a career."

After working briefly at a salon in nearby Mills River, Judy set up business in the converted garage, where she was quickly joined by Frankie. Their salon may be plain on the outside, but inside you feel like you're in the middle of an Easter egg. The walls are pink with plum trim. And the windows are adorned with lacy print curtains.

Many of their customers are older women who come every week for a wash-and-set. "Fridays are a madhouse here," Frankie says. "Judy has six women before noon. One of 'em is ninety-five years old and can't understand why her hip hurts. Judy has to stop and run and pick her up at her house. If Judy's late, she really gets fussed at."

The sisters also do a brisk business in cuts and styles, aided by a third beautician, thirty-one-year-old Kim Warren, who leads a social life that makes for great discussion. "Kim's the one that gets all the men," Frankie says. "She's younger and prettier."

Judy agrees. "Kim's the most interesting of us 'cause of her boyfriends. She had four dates in one day. I told Frankie, 'That first one's pretty lucky, but I'd hate to be the last.' "

Judy walks over to Betsy, the dryer chair, to check Mrs. Heffner's hair. Mrs. Tully and Mrs. Kowalski are now chatting Yankee-to-Yankee—in other words, so fast that a Southerner can follow their conversation only in snippets. "They're musically inclined," Mrs. Tully is saying. "I don't like it. Johnny sent me a tape of his combo. I put it on in the car, and it was awful."

The beauticians pick up what they want to hear and ignore the rest. "The ladies tell us what their children do, the bad and the good," Judy says. "And we have to hear all about their surgeries. We had this little German lady in here yesterday raising hell

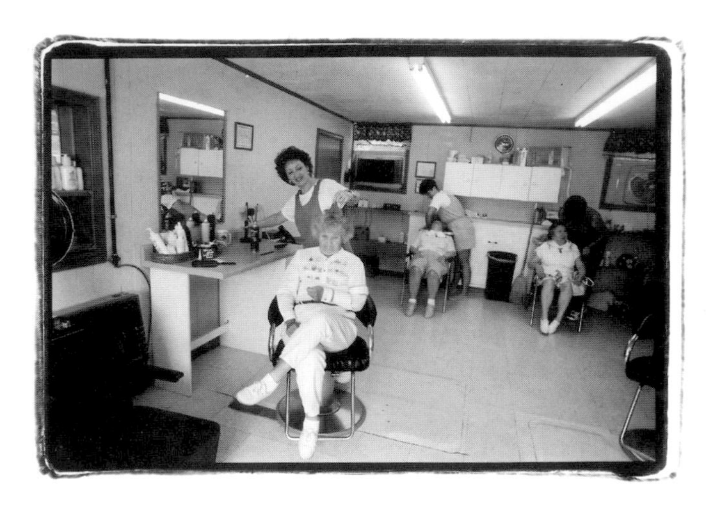

'cause her surgery hasn't healed right. One lady said coming here is her therapy, and it costs a whole lot less than a counselor."

The ladies also talk about their husbands and boyfriends. "We have one customer that'll get out from under the dryer ten times to check and see if her husband's still sitting in the car," Frankie says. "She's afraid he'll sneak down the railroad tracks and call his girlfriend. This lady's eighty-one, and her husband's older than that. If a car horn blows going by her house, she thinks it's his girlfriend. So I blow every time I go by there just for meanness."

Mrs. Tully announces that she's in the midst of a great Dean Koontz novel, and when she's not reading that, she's studying Rush Limbaugh's book and *Reader's Digest.* Mrs. Kowalski, who moved from Chicago to North Carolina ten years ago, tells how her nephew, Robert Kowalski, wrote a best-selling book called *The Eight-Week Cholesterol Diet.*

As Judy puts the finishing touches on Mrs. Kowalski's dark poofy hair, Mrs. Kowalski says she wishes she had a sister. "They're best friends," she says of Frankie and Judy. "They always get along so well."

Mrs. Kowalski then announces that her husband plans to take her out for dinner. "Is it Grove Park Inn or Pizza Hut?" she asks the sisters. Frankie looks at her new hairdo. "Looks like Grove Park to me," she tells Mrs. Kowalski, who tells Judy she'll see her in two weeks and then heads out the door.

Although Friday is Horse Shoe Hair's busiest day, Thursday is more exciting. That's the day when the Southern Railroad train makes its run from Asheville to Brevard, carrying supplies for the paper plant. Every Thursday, Judy, Frankie, Kim, and their customers listen for the train whistle so they can run outside and wave to the railroad men. "Kim blows them kisses," Frankie says.

When time permits, the train stops, and the engineer and his buddies bring Diet Cokes and candy to the beauty parlor ladies. "Last Thursday they had six and a half hours to kill, so they sat here and talked to the ladies all day," Frankie says. "I even worked one in for a haircut."

The railroad guys aren't the beauty shop's only male customers. Frankie and Judy often cut their ladies' husbands' hair. And sometimes one of the migrant farm workers comes in and asks for a trim.

"Kim cut one of the Mexicans that work in the field," Frankie says. "She cut his hair, and it got to all sticking out, and his friends started saying, 'Sombrero! Sombrero!' They thought he needed a hat. Kim told him she wasn't going to charge him. He said, 'Why?' and she said, 'Because your hair looks like shit.' "

Mrs. Tully says she prefers female hairdressers "because you can tell them things you can't tell men."

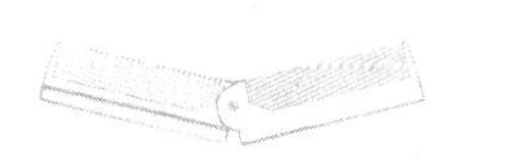

Judy mentions she's also trimmed one of the Mexican men, which sends Frankie into a frenzy of laughter. "Judy kept hollerin' at him, 'YOU WANT YOUR HAIR CUT ABOVE YOUR EARS?' And we said, 'Judy, he's not deaf. He just can't speak English.' "

Because the chitchat rarely lets up in the Horse Shoe salon, mistakes are occasionally made. "We have a lot of customers sit down and we'll be giving 'em a haircut and halfway through they'll say, 'I didn't want a haircut.' And we'll have half their head already done," Judy says.

Offers Frankie, "We dyed one last week, and her hair came out the color of methylate. Somebody grabbed the wrong bottle."

Of the sisters, Judy seems the quieter one. Both women have medium-length auburn-brown hair. Both are on their second marriages. Frankie's husband, David, works at a paper mill. Judy's husband, Troy, is a retired DuPont plant electrician.

The sisters' shop is open Tuesday through Saturday from 9 a.m. "until we get finished," Frankie says. A shampoo-and-set costs $9, and a permanent $38 or $43 if you want the conditioner.

Her hair dry, Mrs. Heffner emerges from under Betsy and waits for her comb-out. Although she says she's retired, Mrs. Heffner and her husband, who once ran a dairy farm, still put in long days growing vegetables and raising cows.

Mrs. Heffner gets her hair done every other week and remembers the days when bimonthly shampoos were considered an extravagance. "In the old days there wasn't enough water to wash your hair so much," she says. "You had to get it out of the well or the spring and carry it in buckets and light a fire to heat it."

"Your curl is so pretty, Lucille," Frankie tells Mrs. Heffner. As she prepares to leave, Mrs. Tully says she prefers female hairdressers "because you can tell them things you can't tell men." With that, she waves good-bye and roars off in her champagne-colored Cadillac.

"We have a good time here," Frankie says, watching her go. ■

In the land that inspired *The Andy Griffith Show,* the beauty parlors are filled with ladies like Aunt Bee, who gossip while pretending to hate gossip, and then go home to cook supper for their beloved Andys, Gomers, Goobers, and Barneys. In places such as Beverly's One Stop Beauty Shop in Hendersonville, North Carolina, husbands often sit on the couch behind the hair dryers while their wives get poufed up like Thelma Lou on a Saturday night. And with any luck, their hair will still be good as new come time to go to Sunday school.

Beverly's One Stop Beauty Shop

HENDERSONVILLE
NORTH CAROLINA

Like many of the finest beauty shops across the Deep South, Beverly's, owned by Beverly Yurth, doesn't look like much from the outside. But the hairdos that come out of the place are first-rate, and the ladies who wear them are funny and fun-loving.

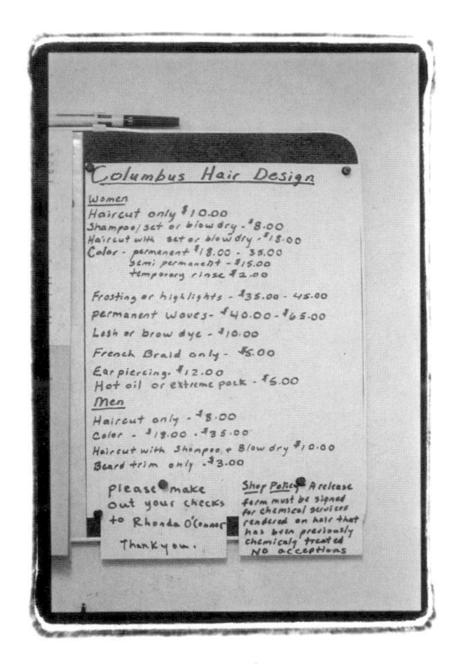

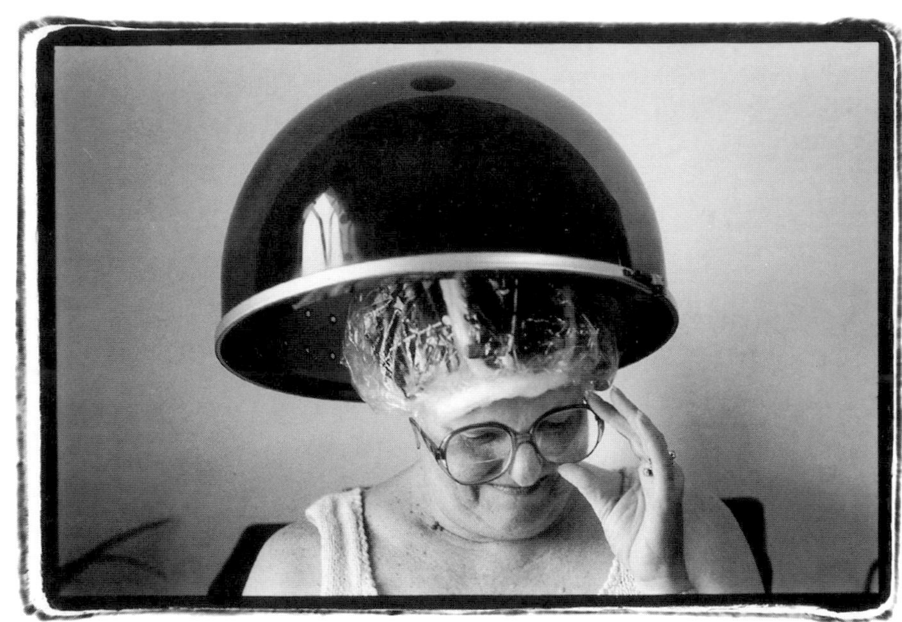

Columbus Hair Design

COLUMBUS NORTH CAROLINA

In Columbus Hair Design on Main Street in Columbus, North Carolina, ladies (and gents) can order from a menu that includes cuts, curls, permanent waves, and even ear-piercing. Most of the ladies are content to get a wash-and-set and then do a little reading under the dryer.

Lovely Lady Styling Salon

COLUMBUS NORTH CAROLINA

In the quaint little dwelling that houses the Lovely Lady Styling Salon, nobody expects to look like the posters on the wall, but it's not for a lack of trying.

In Columbus, North Carolina, being a beauty parlor operator isn't just a right, it's a privilege.

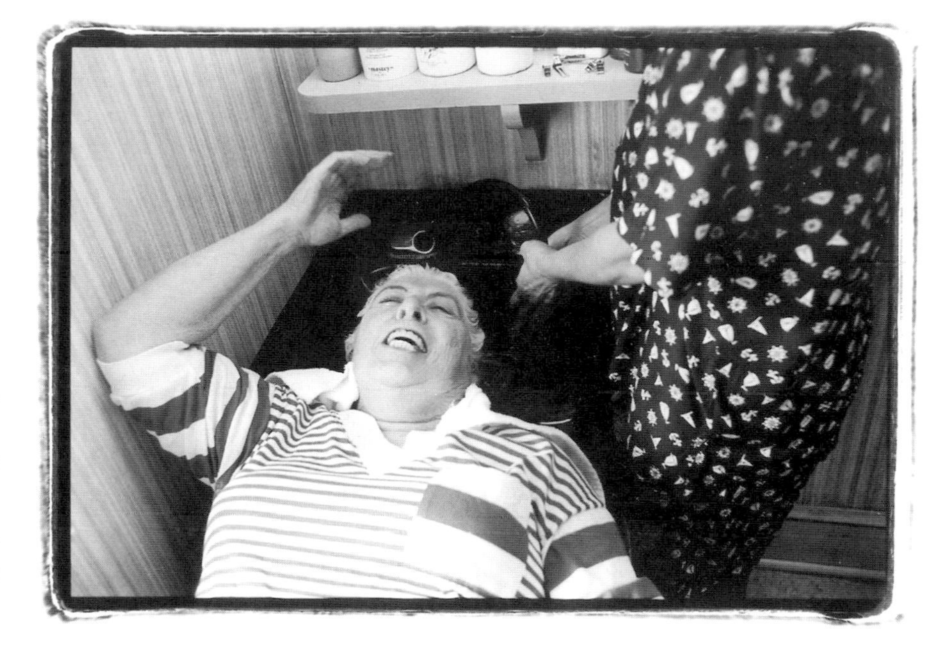

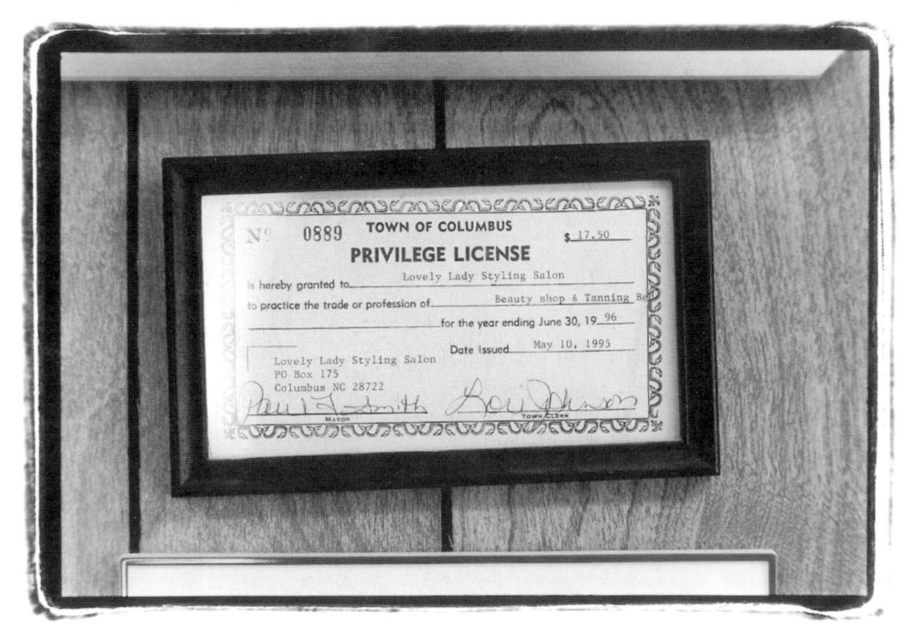

Corner Market Hair Salon

ETOWAH NORTH CAROLINA

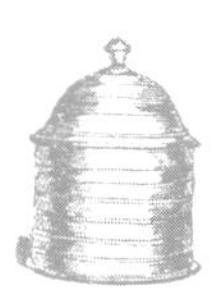

At Corner Market Hair Salon a customer heats her hair under the dryer, which is cooled by the window air conditioner.

Most of the ladies take the time to shop for some fruit and vegetables before they leave the salon.

Left: Husbands can shop for melons next door while their wives get beautiful in Corner Market Hair Salon. Or they can sit a spell in one of the rockin' chairs set invitingly by the grocery door.

Often, in the midst of getting her hair done, a lady will leap clean out of her chair just to put her dibs on an eye-catching watermelon.

Pickled
Eggs
$6.50
ROASTED
PEANUTS
NO SALT
PECAN
LOG
ROLL
RBS
Pinto

Fletcher Hair Design

FLETCHER
NORTH CAROLINA

At Fletcher Hair Design customers drop their change into a jar in an effort to raise money for a friend's liver transplant. But even with that sad reminder of the fragility of life, the ladies take every opportunity to chat and laugh. Age may slow down some of them, but it can't keep them from their weekly wash-and-set appointments.

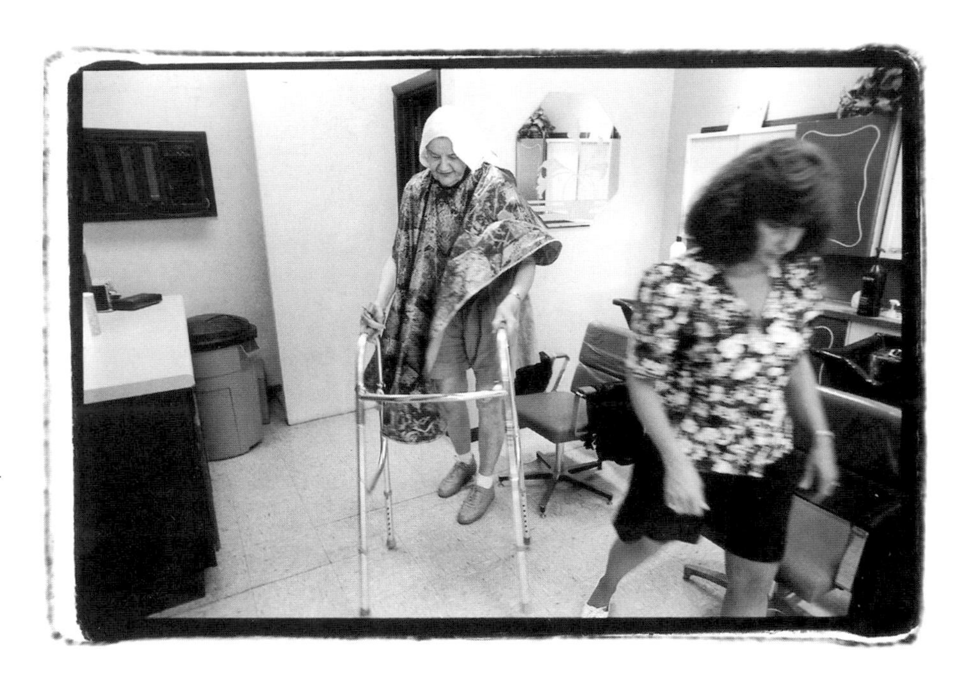

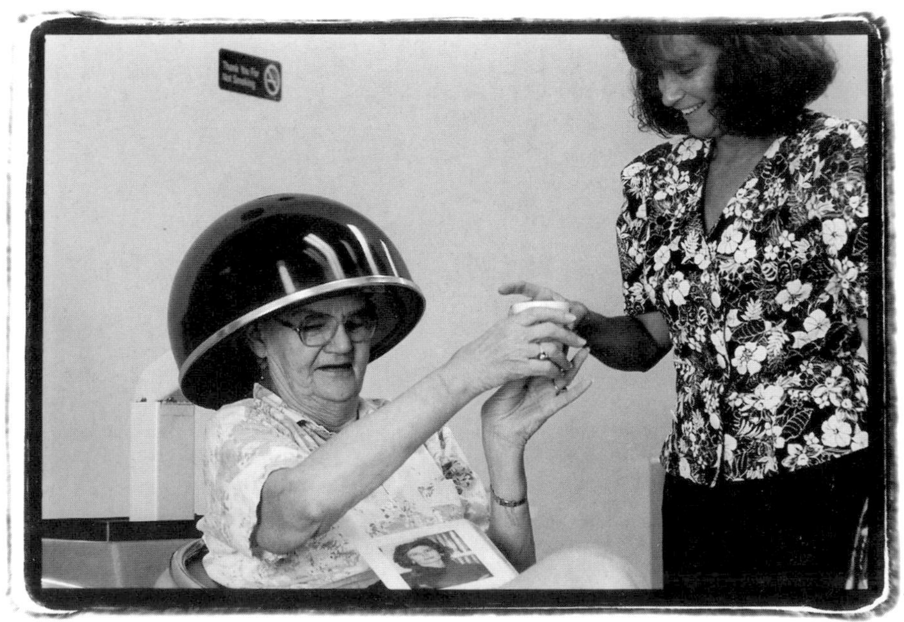

Oak Hill Court Beauty Shop

HENDERSONVILLE NORTH CAROLINA

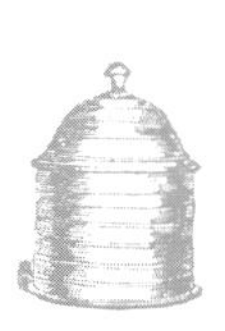

If Oak Hill Court Beauty Shop looks like home, it's because it is. Beauty parlor operator Vernia Hill lives in and works out of her clapboard house.

Misty
NATIONAL
Examiner
Tammy Faye:
JAIL
WILL
SAVE
MY
HUSBAND
ELVIS
Marilyn Monroe
• His love child
• His suicide plan
• The day he killed a man
MARCIA CLARK & CHRIS DARDEN
What
really
happened
during the affair
5 SUREFIRE WAYS
TO MAKE BIG
BUCKS AT HOME

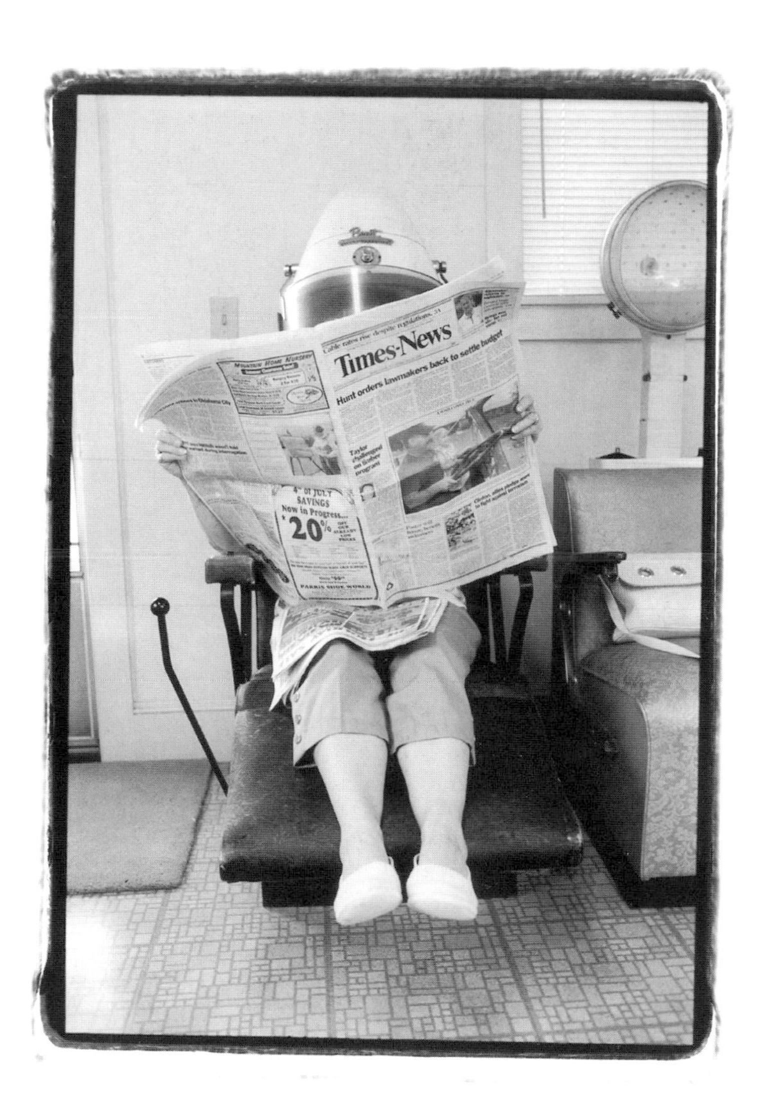
Times-News
Hunt orders lawmakers back to settle budget

Brandon's Beauty and Style Salon

■

SPARTANBURG
SOUTH CAROLINA

Catherine Brandon is famous for tending to the beauty needs not only of her regular salon customers but also of the sick, the infirm, and the down-on-their-luck. And when a customer's luck just flat runs out, Mrs. Brandon heads to the funeral home with an armful of hot oils and curling utensils.

"I did five dead ladies in the last month," she says as she works on a gray-haired woman who, though a bit tired looking, seems in no immediate danger of passing on over to the other side. "I don't mind doin' dead ladies. They're the easiest kind to work with. They don't feel nothin', so you can just do what you want to with 'em. But you try to make 'em look pretty."

Standing at her station in Brandon's Beauty and Style Salon, which she has owned and operated since 1957, Mrs. Brandon combs out the gray-haired woman, Helen Dean, and then hands her a purple fly swatter. Mrs. Dean smokes a cigarette and shoos away flies, which in summer are more numerous than customers in the yellow brick building on South Church Street, near Spartanburg's quaint downtown.

Part of the charm of Brandon's is that it has nothing in common with those newfangled, fancy-pants, walk-in salons.

"Last year somebody broke in and stole the air conditioner, so on hot days we keep the door open," explains Mrs. Brandon, who not only runs the business but is the sole operator. Her daughter, Angela Brandon, is enrolled in the Piedmont Beauty School and plans to join her mother's shop after she graduates.

When Angela moves in, Mrs. Brandon plans to do a little fixin' up. Right now, the salon looks like an old woman in desperate need of a wash-and-set and a manicure. In the front waiting area, the vinyl couches sag almost to the worn beige tile floor. Most of the ladies, therefore, sit in the green vinyl hair-dryer chairs, even as they wait to be washed and curled.

The hair dryers have been in business as long as Mrs. Brandon, but they clearly haven't fared as well. One helmet is held together with duct tape. Yet part of the charm of Mrs. Brandon's shop is that it has nothing in common with those newfangled, fancy-pants, walk-in salons, where the tips can exceed what she charges for a perm.

The paneled walls in Brandon's are covered with little sayings—some on store-bought plaques, others handwritten with a magic marker on yellowing index cards. "The hurrier I go, the behinder I get" reads a message above Mrs. Brandon's workstation. "Keep your words soft and sweet, just in case you have to eat them" warns another.

On the walls, too, hang dog-eared posters that advertise products designed especially for the magnificently coifed black women depicted in the ads. "With hair so beautiful, it has to be Lovely" reads one promoting potions by Lovely

Products of Mauldin, South Carolina.

"I only work with colored hair," Mrs. Brandon says, and she's not talking about Lady Clairol. "My daughter can handle both. But when I went to school, if you were colored, you learned colored hair, if you were white, you did white hair. That was in the forties. I had to go to Atlanta to go to school 'cause they weren't giving colored lessons here. You had to go out of town to get your courses.

"Colored hair's different from white hair. It looks kinky and nappy, but it's not. It's more delicate than people think it is. Some of that stuff white folks put on their hair will make ours fall out."

Mrs. Brandon's anachronistic views extend way beyond the world of hair, which thirty-three-year-old Bernard Leak discovers as his girlfriend, Louise Love, gets her hair curled. Leak makes the mistake of expressing pleasure that the Citadel now accepts female cadets. "Those days when you think a woman can't do things are over," Leak says. "I believe there'll be a woman president."

"I like to come in here 'cause I like the smell of it," Leak says. "But I get my hair cut at Pete's Barber Shop."

Mrs. Brandon's hands stop moving. She looks sternly at Leak. "That'll be the end of the world," she declares. "A woman ought to stay in a woman's place. You get more respect that way. Now you get on a bus, and the men won't get up for you."

Leak, a Spartanburg printer, figures it's a good time to change the subject. "I like to come in here 'cause I like the smell of it," he says. "But I get my hair cut at Pete's Barber Shop."

Suddenly Mrs. Brandon thinks he's the sexist one. "You stay here and I'll have you slicked and curled and everything else," she warns, and then turns to Louise Love. "Okay, Honey, you sit over there about thirty minutes, and then I'll rinse you out."

Born in 1930, when women's lib and civil rights were beyond imagination in the Deep South, Mrs. Brandon grew up at 280 Sims Avenue in one of Spartanburg's black neighborhoods. Her father, Emanuel Boyd, was a

construction worker and cement finisher. Her mother, Flossie, stayed home to raise eight children.

Young Catherine's favorite thing, growing up, was to plait the hair on her dolls. After she finished Spartanburg's Carver High School in 1948, she went to the Apex Beauty School in Atlanta, then returned to Spartanburg to set up shop in 1949.

"Hair is the only thing I ever did, after I finished school," Mrs. Brandon says. On the walls in her tiny work cubbyhole hang her licenses, diplomas, and certificates, including one proclaiming her a graduate of "The Cold Wave Curl Clinic" held at the Spartanburg Holiday Inn on November 4, 1983.

A woman walks through the back door, which opens onto the gravel parking lot, to ask Mrs. Brandon and the other ladies if they'd like to order barbecue for lunch, with courtesy delivery from a nearby church that's holding a fundraising cookout. The women place their orders. Mrs. Brandon participates in the barbecue discussion and subsequent miscellaneous yakking while scooping Demyias hair dress and conditioner from a jar and massaging it through a customer's hair.

She doesn't have time to stop working and visit because a half-dozen ladies are lined up in the dryer chairs, waiting for her services. The old black rotating fan that sits on a table in her workstation blows hot air on the beautician and her customer. And with the back door propped open, flies aren't the only things that invite themselves in.

A retiree in a white pork-pie hat and a matching golf shirt helps himself to a Coke from the cooler by the door and then settles down for a visit with Mrs. Brandon. "I was cleaning up a while ago and found some money," he tells her. "Mama hides that stuff all over the house."

"She's my friend," Long says, "and I stop in here every now and then and check on her."

"I know," Mrs. Brandon tells him, "her mind kind of comes and goes." The man, Donald Long, a former builder who keeps busy in retirement delivering Domino's Pizza, continues his report on Mama. "She messed up that rug in her house so she could get new carpet all over the place. She don't realize you can't keep living high on the hog, not at her age."

Mrs. Dean still holds the purple fly swatter as she sits under the hair dryer, reading a *Jet* magazine. Long says "Hey!" to her and the other ladies and announces he has a half-hour to kill before he reports to Domino's. Busy as she is, Mrs. Brandon seems delighted with his company. She'd probably be delighted to see him even if he didn't insist on bragging about her to anyone who'll listen.

"She's a good woman," Long says. "One of the best in the neighborhood. If she wasn't married, I'd marry her myself. She's my friend, and I have to stop in here every now and then and check on her."

Long's nickname is "Kojak," and he earned it for obvious reasons. He doesn't need Mrs. Brandon's professional services, or for that matter even a barber's. He has a friend, though, a man named Larry, who has sworn off barbers as long as Mrs. Brandon's in business.

"These younger men, they like their hair fixed, like the women do," Long says. "Catherine's the kind who can't say no to anybody. She does shut-ins, handicapped, and dead people, too. I don't know how she does those dead people. And she'll do these ladies that look dead, only they're sleeping in the beauty chair. I don't know how she does it. But that's why everybody's crazy about her."

While Mrs. Brandon works, her friend, Florence Ferguson, answers the telephone and facilitates much of the shop conversation. Since she retired

from the medical center, Mrs. Ferguson, sixty-eight, spends much of her time at Brandon's, where the real-life dramas are almost as entertaining as those on TV.

"Oh, Honey, we talk about everything you can imagine," Mrs. Ferguson says. "I been knowing Cat since we were kids. She does my hair every two weeks. That's how often most of the ladies come in. We gossip and watch TV. Oh, we have a good time. We love wrestling, and *Guiding Light.* We got TVs everywhere in here."

At age sixty-six, Mrs. Brandon seems not a bit interested in leaving the beauty business, even though her husband, Aubrey Brandon Jr., has long been retired from his job doing car body repair. Although he rarely sets foot in the beauty shop, Aubrey Brandon isn't opposed to a little beautifying. "I came home one day and there was this black stuff all over the place," Mrs. Brandon says. "He'd done tinted his hair. But it looked good on him, sure 'nough.

"I'm pretty good at color myself. Some others don't know how to do it. White hair'll turn yellow if you don't tone it down. They don't teach 'em that in school. And that's what they need to know. In school, they give 'em too much pencil work. You got to get into it with your fingers."

The Brandons have three children (their fourth, a little boy, was killed in a bicycle accident when he was nine years old) and seven grandchildren, whose photographs decorate the beauty shop's shelves and walls. On Sundays they all attend the Macedonia Baptist Church. Mondays, Mrs. Brandon pays the bills.

"I got too many ladies need fixin' for me to go gettin' retired," Mrs. Brandon. "Used to, I had all these booths in here rented out. But all them others are gone. I'm the only one doin' hair. I'm happy to be alone, 'til my daughter comes."

She finishes curling Louise Love, a thirty-five-year-old cleaning-company supervisor, who's been a Brandon's customer for years. "She's the only one can do my hair," Miss Love says. "I love coming here. Everybody talks about what's going on. I've heard some good stories sitting in this chair."

Mrs. Brandon laughs. "My customers tell me stuff. Like if they've had a quarrel or something, they ask if I think they're right. We talk about the old times, how things done changed, how prices changed and keep on changing." Her prices haven't changed as much as some. She charges $25 to $35 for a permanent and $15 for a wash-and-set, which includes a conditioning treatment.

"I don't have any walk-ins," says Mrs. Brandon, who, on average, tends to ten customers a day, Tuesdays through Saturdays. "I imagine it's all right for them other places. But they don't know their customers like I do. You got to know what they've had on their head. 'Cause if you don't know, and you go to messin' with it, their hair's gonna all fall out."

As she works, Mrs. Brandon looks every bit the professional. She wears white pants, a white smock, and rubber gloves. Her own gray hair could use a wash-and-set, she says. Soon enough, her daughter will come around to do it.

The fly-swatter lady, Mrs. Dean, forty-nine, who works in a local grocery store, is just about ready to leave. She's had her hair washed, curled, and conditioned with pressing oils. "You got to straighten it before you can curl it," Mrs. Brandon explains. Mrs. Dean nods and looks in the mirror. "Catherine's the best, as far as I'm concerned," she says.

The barbecue sandwiches arrive. The ladies eat and talk. Mrs. Brandon works between bites. Pleasant and grandmotherly, she speaks only of nice things, such as the weather and the new BMW plant and her friends at the nursing home.

"A dog has lots of friends because he wags his tail instead of his tongue" reads one of her little sayings. Her favorite saying isn't on the wall, but she knows it by heart and is happy to recite it. "If you can't say something nice about somebody, then don't say nothin'. Or at least don't say it too loud." ■

South Carolina is home to Charleston, one of the great cities of the Old South, and therefore home as well to many great Southern ladies. Away from that charming coastal town, along isolated blacktops and down dirt roads, Carolina women still want to be beautiful. At the Hidden Beauty Styling Salon in Inman, the building looks more like an abandoned gas station. But the inside could serve as the set for *Steel Magnolias,* complete with colorful characters hugging and kissing each other.

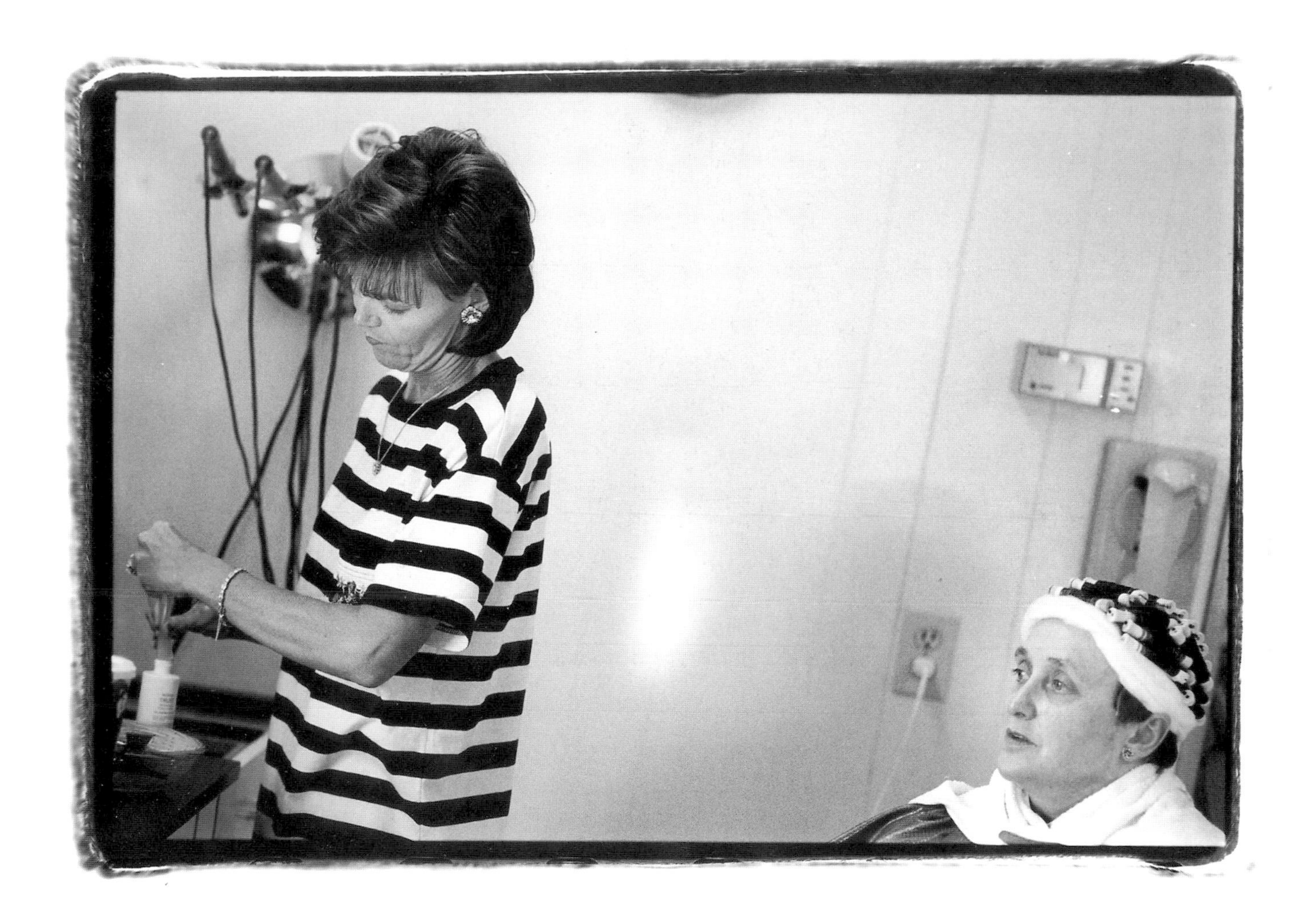

Hidden Beauty Styling Salon

INMAN
SOUTH CAROLINA

■ *Sometimes becoming beautiful entails a few anxious moments on the part of the customer. Inside Hidden Beauty a stylist prepares a potion for the head of a lady who appears to have just emerged from brain surgery, taped and sewn back together.*

Scissors Palace

INMAN
SOUTH CAROLINA

■ *You can't play the slot machines at Scissors Palace, but the customers like to joke that a visit here is almost as pleasant as a trip to Vegas.*

The beauty parlor becomes a waiting room for males of all ages, who pass the time under a hair dryer as their dream lady gets beautified. In Scissors Palace they could pass the time faster if they'd volunteer for sweeping duty.

Spartan Beauty Square

SPARTANBURG
SOUTH CAROLINA

Even on busy days, the pace is slower than a Southern drawl in Spartan Beauty Square. Because the customers have all been coming here for years, there's no need to repaint the original sign on the side of the building. Everybody knows by heart what it says.

A good beautician learns early on how to do hair while talking on the telephone.

At Spartan Beauty Square a customer waits for her own chance for conversation with the operator. If only the walls could talk. . . .

My only license
is Cosmetologist...
the rest are
just sidelines!

A Bad Hair Day.

Bad
Hair
Day!

THE HAIR STYLIST
"Just do me like her"
Hairdresser
I am a Beautician,
Not a magician

Bad Hair Day!
©1994 LA SWEATS

Hollywood Designs

(formerly Atkins Barber & Beauty Salon)

■

MEMPHIS
TENNESSEE

Step inside the hippest hair salon in Memphis and the first thing you see is eighty-six-year-old Riley Shumaker, who's reclining in a red-cushioned barber chair waiting for his next customer.

"I was off sick for a while, so things are still a little slow," he says. A soft-spoken man, he has to holler to make himself heard above the rockabilly music blaring from a speaker above his head.

Just as Riley opens the morning newspaper, in walks a fellow whose outfit suggests Grandpa Jones on court at Wimbledon—white T-shirt, white shorts hitched up by black suspenders, black socks, and scruffy black tennis shoes. But Otis Allen is no Andre Agassi pretty-boy tennis player. He's a semiretired farmer in need of a trim. Allen tells Riley to give him the works—that is, a shave and a haircut.

This is not an especially arduous task considering Allen has worn his brown hair short, like newly mowed grass, and parted down the middle for going on forty-five years,

which is exactly how long he's been coming here every other week for a shave and a trim.

Neither Riley nor Allen is particularly hip, except in that peculiar way the extremely unhip can seem to be (because of their very unhipness) the coolest cats around. In any event, after lathering Allen with shaving cream, Riley commences to work with one of those stainless-steel straight razors, which lends an air of danger to the scene in that it looks for a moment as if the barber's about to slit the throat of a most loyal customer.

"Things are still a little slow," says Riley.

"This used to be called Atkins Barber Shop, and that's what my customers still call it," says Riley, a one-time farmer from Mississippi who switched to barbering in the 1950s. "After Robin bought the place, she put up all these pictures of Elvis and put in the music and changed the name to Hollywood Designs, I think it is. Up here in the front, we still call it Atkins."

Allen (who gives his age as "old enough to know better and still young enough to want to") can't resist chiming in, even with the razor scraping away at his throat. "I wouldn't be caught dead back yonder in that other part."

He's talking about the middle and largest section of this storefront salon, where owner Robin Tucker, thirty, is famous for turning out cool, retro hair designs, such as the modified Elvis pompadour she's sporting at the moment. It's "at the moment" because Robin's hair changes almost as fast as those rockabilly songs she plays on the newly installed sound system.

The Memphis native, who's been doing cool coiffures for thirteen years, bought the old Atkins Barber & Beauty Salon after she saw it little more than a year ago and went crazy with the possibilities.

At the time, Atkins—which had boomed with business through the 1940s, '50s, and '60s—was still an untouched relic of a shop, with Riley buzz-cutting the retirees in the front and two beauticians, Ruth Cook and Alice Hollingsworth, tending to the weekly wash-and-set ladies in the attached beauty parlor.

Robin wasn't interested in shaving retirees or poofing up little old ladies, but she fell in love with the place nevertheless. "I looked in the window, and I thought, 'Man, this is so cool.' I just love this fifties stuff," she says, pointing out the original chrome-trimmed, vinyl-padded chairs at the beauty shop's seven workstations, which are separated by 3-foot-high walls of glass block.

Because the shop was so authentically fifties when she bought it, Robin hasn't had to install any period reproductions. Instead she's given the walls a fresh coat of green paint that is anything but institutional. And she's added other eye-catching touches, such as her own still-life photographs, as well as old black-and-whites of long-forgotten prizefighters, country-and-western singers, ballroom dancers, and marching bands.

"He's my main man," says Robin about Elvis, her idol and hairstyling inspiration.

And, of course, there's the ever-present Elvis, who—although still occasionally spotted at Burger King or Kmart—seems to have settled into his new role as Robin's idol and hair-styling inspiration. "He's my main man," the stylist says.

She didn't know it when she came across Atkins Barber & Beauty Salon, but Robin quickly found out that her aunt used to work here in the 1950s and '60s and counted Elvis's wife, Priscilla, among her regular customers. "My mom told me that when she was pregnant with me, she was the receptionist here," Robin says. "My aunt was doing the beehive on Priscilla. I don't remember it, but I used to hang out here."

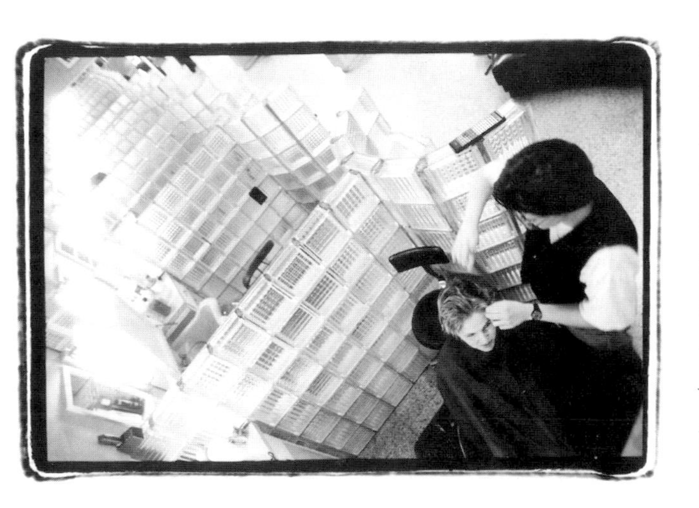

In those days other music celebrities were also regulars. Gospel singer Al Green's mother had her wigs done at Atkins. And soul man Isaac Hayes brought in his girlfriend when she needed beautifying.

That such famous folks frequented the shop decades ago seems especially appropriate, what with Robin being no stranger to modern-day celebrities. After graduating from Overton High School of Performing Arts in 1984 and then beauty school a year or two later, Robin worked in another Memphis salon and decided she didn't like cutting hair.

The problem, she discovered, wasn't that she didn't like cutting hair, but that she didn't like cutting hair the way she was cutting it in that particular Memphis salon. Robin found her calling a few years later when Hollywood came to town to turn the life story of cousin-marryin',

piano-poundin' native son Jerry Lee Lewis into a movie called *Great Balls of Fire!* Robin hired on as a freelance makeup artist assigned to work on the extras.

"The producers kept trying to hire people to do fifties-style crew cuts, pompadours, flattops, and D.A.s, and everybody kept doing these eighties styles. So I told 'em, 'That's my forte. Let me do it.' In one day, I bet I did a thousand crew cuts, and I was doin' all the other cool stuff. That's when I really got turned on to hair."

She did hair for other movies, including the Tom Cruise blockbuster *The Firm,* as well as the television show *Elvis and Me.* That led to work with local music promoters, who called her to work on some of rock 'n' roll's most famous heads.

"I've done Metallica, Def Leppard, Guns N' Roses, the B-52s, Bette Midler, and Paul and Linda McCartney. They usually get their hair done the last hour before they go onstage, so I go to the Liberty Bowl or wherever they're performing. Most of them are really nice. Paul McCartney, the biggest star in the world, had no attitude at all. I did his makeup and styled his hair. He didn't really need a trim."

One performer who needed more than a trim was Guns N' Roses's mercurial lead singer, Axl Rose, who appeared before Robin with his flowing red tresses matted in road grit. "Man, I couldn't touch him," she says. "I made him take a bath. It was weird because I met his sister, who's his promotional director, and she's like some kind of sorority girl. She's so nice. And then you've got him.

"Axl was just really uptight. He was trying to get everything ready. There was a lot of foul language. The concert was on Elvis's death date, and Axl wanted the person who introduced him to look like Elvis. So I had to get a wig from one of his backup singers and cut it into a pompadour. And the whole time he was fighting with his backup singer because it was like a $450 wig."

While Robin worked on Rose, the singer's then-bandmate—that leather-clad, snake-loving, multi-pierced, guitar-playing, mop-headed fellow named Slash—sauntered in. "He's got that cigarette hanging out of his mouth. He's like, 'Whatcha gonna do for me?' I'm like, 'Man, I

can't do anything for you.' I mean, what are you going to do?"

At Hollywood Designs, Robin is the Sassoon-trained master stylist. Instead of hiring more stylists, she recruits her young assistants right out of beauty school so she can train them herself. Her clientele is heavy on young hip professionals like Kai Lee, twenty-six, a sales consultant, who's followed Robin all over the place for a half-dozen years.

"I wouldn't consider having my hair done by anybody else," says Ms. Lee, who will leave Hollywood Designs this morning with her brown hair in a short, swingy 'do that perfectly complements her little black-and-white checkered skirt, clingy white top, and stylishly small bronze eyeglasses. "Robin understands my lifestyle."

"I've been coming here every Saturday since the 1950s."

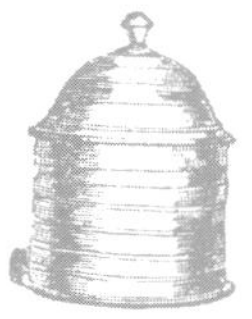

To her credit, Robin also understands that there's still a sizable population that wants crew cuts and wash-and-sets. That's why Riley Shumaker still holds court in the front room of Hollywood Designs, and Ruth Cook and Alice Hollingsworth still do shampoos-and-sets in the back.

Red-headed Ruth, like Riley, is accidentally hip, in that she wears pink polyester pants, pink knit tops, and sensible shoes—and she means it. Tuesdays through Saturdays for nearly twenty-two years, Ruth—who declines to give her age, but describes herself as "a stout ol' gal"—has presided over the back room like some kind of trailer-park Oprah, regaling her ladies with countryfied jokes and stories and even listening to theirs when she needs to catch her breath.

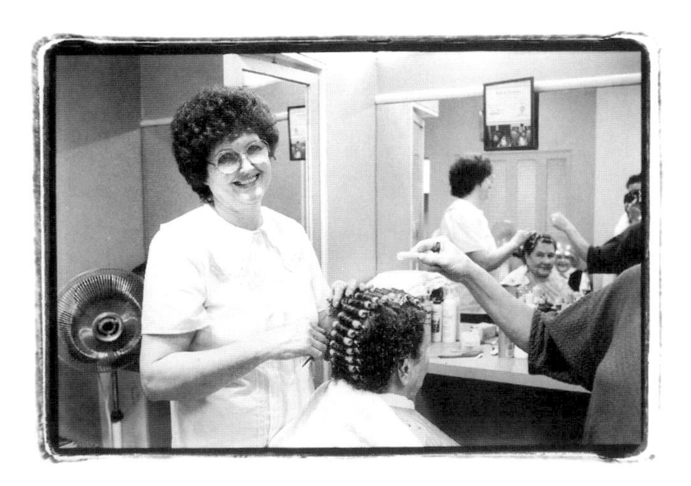

"Ruth is very entertaining, and she don't make you sit and wait to get combed out and do all those other things people do nowadays," declares seventy-eight-year-old Olive Daugherty, who has just emerged from under the dryer. "She don't rob you either. Her prices are very competitive, and she doesn't expect a handout."

"Keep talkin' nice about me, Olive," Ruth says as she undoes the rollers in Mrs. Daugherty's hair. Alice, meanwhile, stuffs toilet paper behind the ears of another lady who's about to go under the dryer. "Ruth, am I getting too black?" yells a woman who's reared back with her head in the sink.

"I been coming here every Saturday since the 1950s, and I love the association with all these old folks," continues Mrs. Daugherty, whose husband, Robert, is at this very moment shooting the breeze up front with Riley the barber. "We're all old folks these days. The younger ones wash it every day and go out with it wet. Every two months they'll come and let Robin cut it."

Ruth and her ladies are amused and fascinated by Robin and her staff and clientele. "I couldn't wear my hair like they do, but I get a kick out of it, and them, especially Robin. She just kills me," Ruth says. "And I just love all that Elvis stuff. In fact I had tickets to go see Elvis when he up and died. My sister called me and told me. I said, 'He has not.' She said, 'Turn on the TV.' And right there it was."

One of Ruth's ladies pipes up and says, "I was in the drugstore when I heard it."

In the heyday of Atkins Barber & Beauty Salon, Ruth and Alice did their setting and curling in the center room that Robin and her young assistants took over when Robin bought the business. Ruth and Alice, whose clientele had been slowly dwindling over the years, settled in the small back room crammed with a couple of sinks and old dryers.

With Robin working so hard to improve the looks of things, Ruth dropped more than a few hints that she liked the color orange. The walls in the back room remained mustard yellow, but Robin took Ruth's hints to heart and installed the wildest, orangest thing the wash-and-set ladies had ever seen.

"I figured she was gonna put me an orange flower in here, and she come and put this up," Ruth says, pointing to the room's predominant decoration—a large orange, New-Agey, cloth wall hanging decorated with pictures of the planets and stars. "People say we look like a bunch of fortune-tellers back here," Ruth complains. "I told Robin I could make me a dress out of that thing."

Originally from Light, Arkansas, about 120 miles northwest of Memphis, Ruth held a variety of jobs before she found her true calling in the beauty business. "First job I ever had was picking cotton," she says. "Man, I can pick them whiteballs. I got them fat hands. Then I worked at the Ed White Shoe Factory in the bow department. They kept telling me to keep

my mouth shut or the boss man would fire me. Well I've always liked to talk. Sure enough, the old man fired me. I didn't feel too bad 'cause he fired his own wife one time."

Next came a stint at a bathroom-fixtures plant. Ruth's assignment was to put caps on the water faucets. She'd passed through similar jobs at shirt and furniture factories when her husband, Granville, turned to her one day and said, "You're always doin' hair when you're home. Why don't you take you a beauty course? Maybe that's what you'd really like."

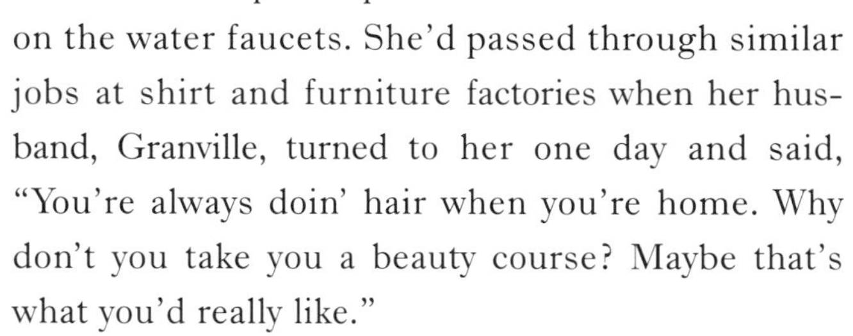

"I told him, 'I never did like book learnin',' " Ruth recalls. "But he said, 'I'll help you get through it.' So anyway, I gave it a try, and this is where I ended up. This is where I got my hair fixed when we first came to Memphis. Back then this place was lined with operators. This girl that worked back here with me did these fluffy, real huge hairdos. My customers mostly wanted your basic wash-and-curl."

One of Ruth's customers, eighty-seven-year-old Kathleen Clayton, who once worked in central service at Memphis Hospital, says the backroom ladies generally discuss the same topics every week. "We talk about hair and church and Hazel that used to work here. We always go over Hazel's case. She's fine now. That stroke didn't affect her much. But she retired. She lives out at the Heritage Place now. Doesn't even have to make her bed."

"That's what I call retired," Ruth agrees.

"Anyway," Mrs. Clayton continues, "I get my hair done every Saturday. The hour might change a little bit. I call Ruth every Thursday, and then I write down the time so I won't be late. I've never been late. I don't believe in being late for anything. You don't work at a hospital for as many years as I did and not learn that."

While the ladies chatter away, a skinny young man as tall as a pro basketball player wanders into the back room, sits down, and smiles. Stevan Lazich, twenty-one, is Robin's 6-foot, 6½-inch receptionist, who today stands closer to 7 feet thanks to a pair of shiny black cowboy boots, size 13. Although a few weeks ago his hair stretched down his back, it's now standing up in a pompadour. He's wearing a gold-trimmed black bowling shirt that says "Mose" over the pocket.

"The ladies are really great," Stevan says, stretching his long legs halfway across the tiny room. "I love to talk to 'em. That's what's so cool about working here. You got the gentlemen in the front, and the ladies in the back, and Robin kicking out all these styles in the middle."

Robin thinks Stevan should go to beauty school, but he sees a career for himself in clothing design. He's especially interested in the vintage look, which is well-suited to the Elvis environment at Hollywood Designs. "He never heard anything like us, the way we rattle," Ruth says, glancing with affection at the pompadoured string bean.

"We talk about hair and church and Hazel that used to work here. We always go over Hazel's case."

In the middle room Robin greets a frizzy-haired, goateed client and says, "So what are you thinking about doing?" After a lengthy back and forth with the man, Robin assigns one of her assistants to shampoo him. The stylist walks toward the door to say good-bye to a regular client, Patty Parks, a forty-four-year-old respiratory therapist who first came here as a ten-year-old.

"I started coming back about six months ago, and it was amazing—everything was the same," says Ms. Parks, whose father is a regular customer of Riley the barber. "I come back about every six weeks now. I want the easiest, quickest thing. I have to leave for work at six in the morning, so I don't have a lot of time for my hair." Robin has Ms. Parks's gray hair in a shoulder-length cut, easy enough to wash and dry every morning.

"I can't imagine going a whole week without washing my hair," Ms. Parks says. "But that's what the older ladies do."

Robin nods. "I know nothin' about shampoos, sets, and froufrous. Men's cuts can be very cool. I've learned a lot from Riley. I'll watch him do a flipper cut and then interpret it for my clients."

Although she expects that one day there will no longer be a need for the Ruths and Rileys of the hair world, Robin seems in no hurry to see them gone from her shop. "As long as they're here, I'm going to keep their stuff the same," she says.

As Robin works on the frizzy-headed man, Riley holds court in the front room with a half-dozen men, including one who's actually in need of his services. With his eyes fully closed and his mouth hanging open, the man appears to be in a sound sleep as the barber clips his thinning hair. "Back yonder, they call this 'stylin',' " Riley says. "I call it a trim." ■

Tennessee holds a special place in beauty parlor history. That's because Nashville, the country music capital of the world, is overflowing with glamorous, immovable, monumental hair. Dolly Parton's bosom may be big, but her hair is insurmountable.

Before she became a country music queen, Tammy Wynette did hair in Midfield Beauty Shop near downtown Birmingham, Alabama. For years after she found success in Nashville, she kept her beauty license up-to-date—something to fall back on, as every good mother likes to say.

But not every Tennessee woman knows the words to "Stand by Your Man." Most are just regular folks, like the ladies at Hair Executives in Fountain City, where Theresa tries to make them feel like superstars.

Elvis Presley, by the way, was no stranger to the beauty parlor. In Memphis he regularly visited the salon to have his light brown wavy hair dyed jet black. And then, we imagine, he retired to Graceland for another peanut butter-and-banana sandwich.

Hair Executives

FOUNTAIN CITY TENNESSEE

In beauty school, one of the things they don't teach you is how to talk on the phone while doing a manicure. But the staff at Hair Executives has no problem performing this balancing act. Once you learn to wield a hair dryer, scissors, and a nail file, it's not difficult to add a telephone to the mix.

Lady B-Lovely Beauty Shoppe

MAYNARDVILLE TENNESSEE

One of the things they apparently do teach you in beauty school is to give your salon a clever name with its own unique spelling—like Lady B-Lovely Beauty Shoppe. But inside the accouterments remain the same—scissors, rollers, brushes, pins, clips, and hair dryers that look like astronauts' helmets. Take us to your leader, please.

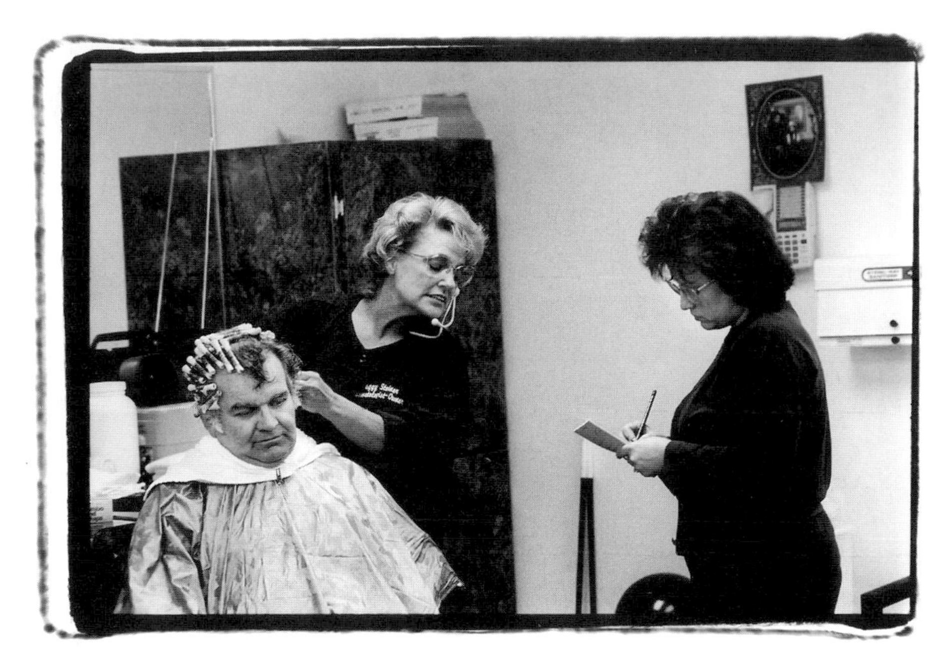

For decades men wouldn't set foot in a beauty parlor, much less enter a place called Lady B-Lovely and settle down for a permanent. But times have changed. Men aren't afraid to reveal their soft sides, even if it involves rollers and Dippity-Do. Here, a fellow tries to look nonchalant while his beauticians discuss what they're planning to serve for Easter dinner. A much-younger fellow (bottom right) waits for his turn in front of the mirror.

Hair Illusions

**SMYRNA
TENNESSEE**

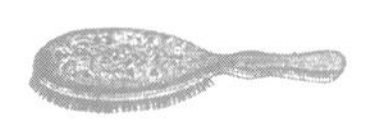

It's a family affair at Hair Illusions, where a grandmother cuddles her bundle of love and a little boy waits while his mama gets trimmed. The shelves are filled with magic potions guaranteed to turn the merely good-looking into the positively lovely. Or is it an illusion?

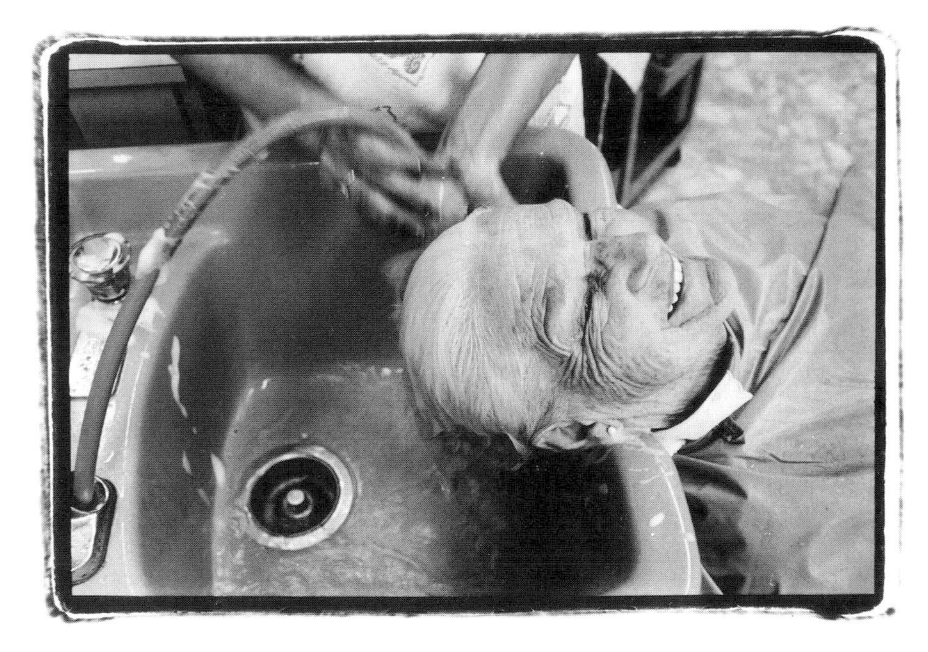

It's an unwritten rule that a good Southern beautician must visit with each customer before, during, and after the hair-doin' event. At Hair Illusions, one of the regulars discusses what she has in mind for her white hair and then gets shampooed so the magic can begin. Two hours later, she's happily out the door. But the good-bye is temporary: Next week, the women meet again—same time, same place.

Special Effects

SMYRNA
TENNESSEE

Even in Tennessee, not every woman can look like Dolly Parton. "I'm a beautician, not a magician" declares a pointed message, to the relief of a customer (top left) who doesn't feel beautiful enough to reveal her big ol' Nashville hairdo. High above the salon's checkerboard floor a pair of clown dolls swing from twin trapezes. But that doesn't mean customers leave looking like Bozo's ex-wives. Most finished hairdos draw big smiles, even on close inspection.

Beauty professionals, including those at Special Effects, enjoy their coffee breaks, which give them a chance to gossip among themselves instead of just with their customers. The gossip, by the way, is never vicious. It sometimes focuses on local big shots, whose thick skins can deflect a little good-ol'-girl chitchat. But mostly the ladies talk about children and grandchildren and each other. When they're not yakking, they hide themselves behind a copy of Southern Living *or* Woman's Day, *or enjoy a bag of chips—cellulite be darned.*

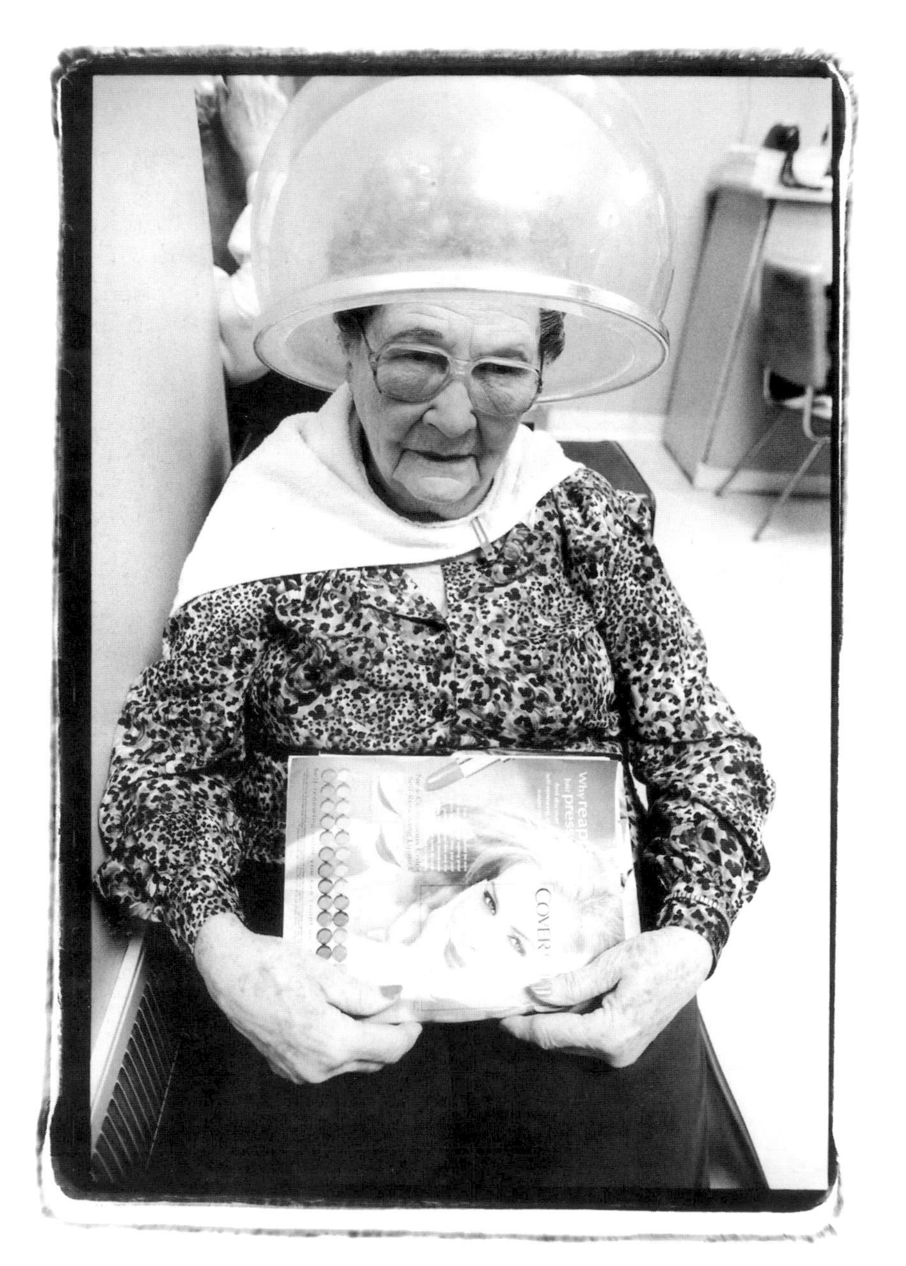

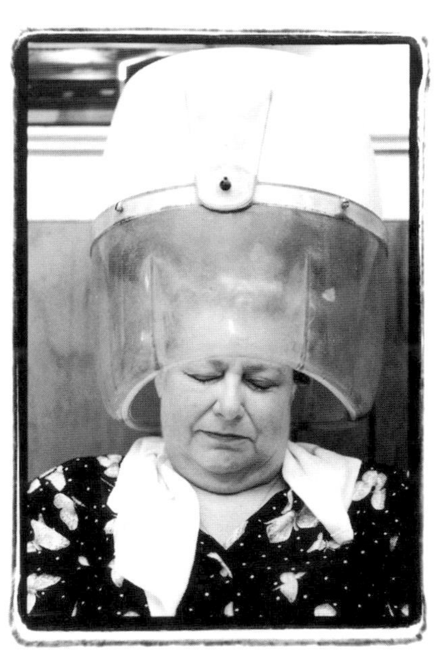

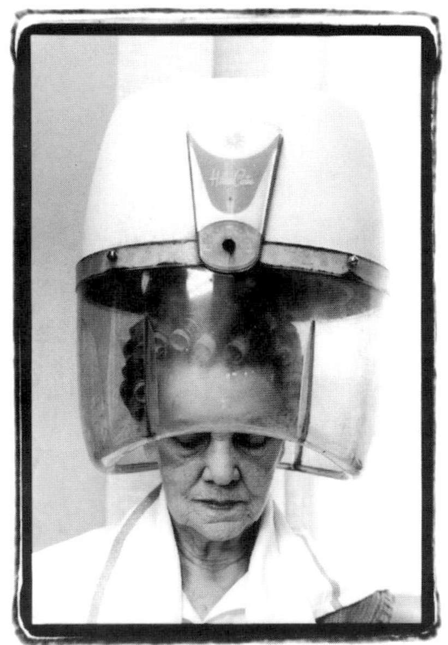

Brazos Barber and Beauty Shop

■

GRANBURY
TEXAS

Delana Holderness stood behind the plate-glass window, staring at the empty sidewalk and street. It was an especially slow morning at Brazos Barber and Beauty Shop, and the sluggishness seemed to extend into the town itself.

Once a cotton farmer's rural paradise, with three cotton gins and a downtown square dotted with mercantile stores, Granbury, Texas, had, in the 1970s, become a picturesque little Western tourist town. A bit of ingenious engineering tapped the nearby Brazos River to create, right inside the city limits, a body of water known as Lake Granbury, which drew a steady stream of artists, retirees, and adventurers, to the raised eyebrows of the local folk.

But even the tourists were out of sight that morning in 1993, as Delana stood behind the plate-glass front window, joined by her brother, Richard Beall, quietly observing the town's sheer deadness. Delana, as now, was a beautician at the shop that her father, Curley Beall, and a partner had opened as a barber shop in the early 1960s.

When Curley turned Brazos Barber Shop into Brazos Barber and Beauty Shop, he figured he was in for a headache.

Richard Beall started barbering at the shop in the mid 1970s, when it was still strictly a man's domain. Back then, farmers and ranchers, some in pointy-toed boots with spurs, told jokes that were, even at the height of women's lib, a bit too salty for the local ladies.

In the late 1970s Curley reluctantly saw the need for a change. His customers, including the manly ranchers, weren't coming in every other week for a crew cut, as had been their custom for decades. Even Richard was letting his hair grow way past his collar, which didn't please Curley at all, but nevertheless helped him see the light.

So Curley turned Brazos Barber Shop into Brazos Barber and Beauty Shop and opened its doors to Granbury's women, including his own daughter, the beautician. But, truth be told, he figured he was in for a headache.

As it turned out, the problems were insignificant and the advantages numerous. By the time Curley died in 1991, just three weeks after his retirement, the beauty side of Brazos was keeping the barber side operational. In fact, there wasn't a single bad side effect from letting in the women. But Curley nevertheless might have been secretly satisfied if he had lived to see what happened that languid morning Delana and Richard stood looking through the front window.

"We were standing real close to the glass, and all of a sudden we heard this huge crash, and bricks just fell in a pile in front of our door," recalls Delana, a petite thirty-nine year old, who wears her dark hair short and feathered forward, to cover her high forehead.

"We see this Cadillac careening across the street. Inside, I could see a head kind of ducked down, and my first thought was somebody was running from the police and had clipped our building. I kept looking, and I realized it was one of my customers, and she was headed right for a house. She ended up smashing into the side of it. She missed the gas main by maybe a foot.

"I ran out the back door, 'cause we couldn't get out the front, and I ran across the street to stop her. Her car had this big ol' piece of insulation from the house sitting on the hood. I said, 'Jessie! Jessie!' She rolled down the window and started saying, 'I'll pay for the damages.' I said, 'Never mind that, are you all right?' "

It turned out that Delana's customer, Jessie Sterling, had suffered a diabetic blackout on the way to her weekly wash-and-set. She sideswiped the shop, then demolished a wing of the house and the front of her Cadillac. No one was hurt, including Jessie, who allowed the paramedics to examine her and then announced she might as well get her hair fixed, seeing as how she was there and had an appointment.

Most of Delana's customers don't seem to mind the masculine origins of the beauty shop.

"She was fine, but I was a basket case," Delana recalls. "I was so nervous I could hardly do her hair. She died a few years after that. Jessie was a real dear lady. My parents went to church with her family."

Like the dear-departed Mrs. Sterling, many of Delana's customers are older ladies who have standing weekly appointments for a wash-and-set. Most don't seem to mind, or necessarily even remember, the masculine origins of Delana's shop, which now services 90 percent women, including seventy-eight-year-old Mary Bachman.

"Delana's been doing my hair for seventeen years," says the Fort Worth-born homemaker, who lived in some of the biggest cities in the United States before settling down in Granbury in 1980. Her husband, Bill, worked for an oil-and-gas trade magazine, and he moved the family to Tulsa, New York City, and Washington, D.C., and then finally back to Texas. ("When I told our friends in

Washington we were moving to a town with a square, they said, 'Oh, we didn't know Bill was a square,' " Mrs. Bachman says.)

"When we lived in New York, I went to Revlon and Sassoon, all those salons on Fifth Avenue. The cab drivers used to tell me I looked real glamorous. But I wasn't that impressed, to tell you the truth," she adds. "I finally ended up going to a neighborhood shop. I think you get better service there."

Brazos Barber and Beauty Shop certainly qualifies as a neighborhood establishment, but so does just about every other business in this town of about 4,000, just a half-hour southwest of Fort Worth. The shop is a few blocks from the courthouse and

the popular downtown square, site of the refurbished Granbury Opera House, where tourists flock to the weekly melodramas.

Brazos Barber and Beauty Shop is housed at one end of a red-brick building, and at the other end is another more modern hair salon. Separating the two, and they probably ought to be separated even though Delana says they have their own loyal clienteles, is an insurance company, where customers can seek solace should they suffer a beauty parlor maiming.

Such a thing has never occurred in Brazos, says Richard, who has spent his entire forty-five years in and out of the tiny shop. His father, a career barber, welcomed the three Beall children—Richard, Delana, and their older brother, Gary, now a Chicago chemist—to visit whenever they wanted.

And they did, partly because there was not much else for kids to do back then in such a small, out-of-the-way place. "When we were growing up, all there was for entertainment was the river," says Richard, who spent long summer days fishing and swimming in the cool brown water.

"We had a walk-in theater on the square, and a drive-in theater, and once in a while we'd have a traveling skating show come through, but that was about it. We had to make up our own things to do."

"If you don't like it, you don't have to live here, and I like it," says "Pig" Williams, one of Curley's original haircut customers.

4-H News & Notes

JACK CASKEY

CURLEY BEALL

OUR NEW SHOP IS OPEN FOR BUSINESS AND WE INVITE OUR FRIENDS TO VISIT US.

New Building, New Equipment, Courteous Service

REGULAR HAIRCUTS -- $1.00 FLAT TOPS -- $1.25

NO APPOINTMENTS NECESSARY. JUST DROP IN AS USUAL.

Brazos Barber Shop

Jack Caskey, 421 W. Pearl — Owners — Curley Beall, Granbury, Texas

TELL IT TO THE WOR[LD]

WANT A[DS]

The Brazos Drive-In theater, in fact, is still operational—one of the rare remaining park-and-watch outdoor movie screens in the country. But it's one of the few things in town that has stayed the same.

With the business boom in Dallas/Fort Worth came an influx of people and housing developments like the town had never seen. The addition of the lake only cemented Granbury's growing image as a sweet respite from the hustle and bustle of the encroaching metropolis. And not everybody was pleased.

"It's nothin' but a tourist trap, Baby," declares Elton Garland "Pig" Williams, a lifelong Granbury resident and one of Curley Beall's original haircut customers who has for years been serviced by Richard Beall.

"If you don't like it, you don't have to live here, and I like it," Williams says. "I got two or three people that still speak to me after all these years."

The youngest of five children, Pig grew up on a "li'l' ol' farm" northeast of town. As a child, his job was to keep the pigs away from the corn during gathering season. "All my folks, I mean all of 'em, had nicknames, so they called me 'Pig Minder,' " he says. "After a while, they dropped the 'Minder.' I've been 'Pig' ever since. But it didn't have nothin' to do with my eatin'."

Williams, who is eighty-seven years old and once ran a dry goods shop on the square, remembers the days when a haircut was 25 cents. He was among the first regular customers at Brazos Barber Shop, and unlike some of the other men, he didn't mind a bit when the ladies started coming in.

"No sir," he says, "I've always liked the ladies. Don't have nothin' against them at all. We always respected 'em. 'Course, nowadays, you can say anything at all and it don't make a whole lot of difference."

A widower since 1980, Williams has since been pursued by a few Granbury widows, including some he met in the beauty parlor. With his full head of gray hair and his unflappable wit, he knows how to turn a lady's head. "Trouble is," he says, "when you get eighty-seven, something goes to happenin' to you, if you know what I mean. It's sad, but it's that way."

Williams didn't mind a bit when the ladies started coming in. "I've always liked the ladies. Don't have nothin' against them at all."

At Brazos, Richard laughs at Williams's tales, which the old-timer typically wraps up in a kind of hillbilly poetry, such as "You can't get all the coons up one tree, my daddy used to say."

"Pig knows more about this town than anybody else," says Richard, who tends to the hair of many a customer he inherited from his daddy. Some of the men still insist on a flattop, but just as many want a layered business cut, which tickles Williams no end.

"They call it 'stylin',' but that's just a fancy name for gettin' more money out of you," Pig says. "Me, I just go in, sit down and let Richard have at it. I say, 'Richard, if you cut it, I'll wear it.' "

Williams keeps fairly quiet about Richard's own coiffure, which amounts to a bald top, with a ring of hair on the sides, and an 8-inch-long tail down the back. Twenty years ago, when he still had a full head of hair, the barber wore it down on his shoulders, to the consternation of the older generation.

"Most of the old-timers would say I needed a haircut worse than they did," he recalls.

Richard didn't exactly plan on being a barber. After graduating from Granbury High School, he figured he'd go to barber school so he could support himself while he worked his way through college—he never made it to college. After a brief stint in the construction business, he settled in at Brazos, where Curley—due to Richard's long hair and the general mood of the younger clientele—made him the resident stylist.

Long before Brazos went into the beauty business, a handful of no-nonsense, hands-on farm ladies regularly visited the barber shop to get haircuts manly enough to rival any rancher's.

Richard did his share of flattops and clipper cuts and only once had a near-fatal accident. "In barber school, a lot of winos would come in to get free haircuts. In fact, about half of 'em would come in and sit in your chair and say, 'Oh, I used to be a barber.' So that was real encouraging.

"Anyway, I had one that was pretty drunk one day. They always want to turn around and face you when they're saying something. I was goin' up the back of one man's head with the clippers when he did that, and I just peeled him all the way up to the crown in back."

Richard didn't feel the need to tell the drunk man what he had done. When Richard was finished, the customer thanked him and walked out the door, with a slick stripe running down the middle of his dark hair.

These days, Richard says, the kids actually ask for that kind of haircut, although in more creative variations. "They'll come in and want me to shave a Texas flag into their hair," he says. "One kid had me shave Bart Simpson's face on the back of his head."

While Richard handles the men, Delana and two other beauticians tend to the women—all in the same 25 by 40-foot room, where the primary decoration on the dark paneled walls is a charcoal sketch of a little boy getting his first haircut.

Delana has tried to pretty up the place with a few well-placed antiques and some Southwestern-style decorations in the waiting area. Like her brother, she never expected to end up as a full-time hairdresser. All she ever wanted in life, she says, was to be a wife and mother.

And she got started at that pretty early. When she was barely sixteen, Delana dropped out of Granbury High to marry Dale Holderness, an electrician, and the next year, she gave birth to twins Chris and Jeremy. As a young mother, she decided it wouldn't be a bad idea to get out of the house. A friend suggested she enter beauty school.

"Growing up, I wasn't a bit interested in hair," Delana says. "That's why it's so strange that I ended up doing this. My mother, her name's Clara, she always tried to get me to fix her hair when I was little, like little girls do, but I never cared anything about it. And here I am doing hair. It's weird."

Mrs. Bachman has no qualms about getting beautified in what many locals still consider a barber shop. "You never hear any dirty talk. And I do like that," she says.

Delana worked in several Texas beauty parlors before setting up for business in Curley's shop in the early 1980s. By then Curley and Richard already had a sizable female clientele, and the addition of Delana made it grow only larger.

Just because a woman lives in Texas doesn't mean she has to have hair as big as the state, the beautician points out. The Dallas Cowboy cheerleaders may sport long, flowing tresses, but most of Delana's female customers keep theirs short and simple, like Mrs. Bachman wears her white hair.

According to Mrs. Bachman, Delana's about the best hairdoer in this part of the Lone Star State. She credits Delana with freeing her from the weekly hair-rolling grind. Now after Mrs. Bachman's weekly wash, Delana styles her short permanent with a brush and blow-dryer. "It's so much easier on your hair," Mrs. Bachman says.

"When I lived in Tulsa, I told my hairdresser that I'd like to try blow-drying, but she told me I didn't have that kind of hair," she adds. "Delana is such a better hairdresser than that woman was. I've had several people come up to me and ask where I get my hair done."

Through the years, Mrs. Bachman's husband has been a customer of Brazos, although they're rarely there at the same time. She has no qualms about getting beautified in what many locals still consider a barber shop. "It's a real pleasant place," she says. "You never hear any dirty talk. And I do like that. Richard and the men talk about sports. Half the time I don't know what they're talking about.

"Some of these barber shops aren't so nice. My father, he was a minister, and he stopped going to a place in Fort Worth because they always told such dirty jokes," Mrs. Bachman says. "One day after he left, the barber came to his house to apologize. That's how bad it had gotten."

In Brazos, while the men talk about sports and the weather, the ladies talk about their homes, gardens, and families. Not all their stories are happy. "I have one lady in particular, her son had gotten into drugs real bad and she was wanting some advice," Delana says. "I told her to be patient—not to turn against him, but not to encourage him.

"It's weird. Half the time you feel like a therapist. I think I've gotten pretty good at it, if you want to know the truth. Basically I just listen. If you give too much advice, you're gonna get yourself in trouble."

If the ladies need more emotional support, they also offer something in exchange that male customers seldom do, Delana says. "I get lovely gifts from some of my women customers. At Christmas I try to give my special ones a little something. They give me clothes, flowers, coffee mugs, all kinds of things. Men don't give gifts. But they do give tips. And that's nice too."

"Half the time you feel like a therapist," says Delana. "Basically I just listen. If you give too much advice, you're gonna get yourself in trouble."

Neither of Delana's sons, who are now twenty-two, intend to go into the beauty or barber business. Chris is a computer draftsman. Jeremy works in town as an auto-body technician. Richard tells a similar story about his twenty-two-year-old son, Brandon, and stepdaughter, Sativa, who's seventeen. "I don't think this business ever crosses their minds," he says.

Richard himself occasionally thinks of doing something else for a living.

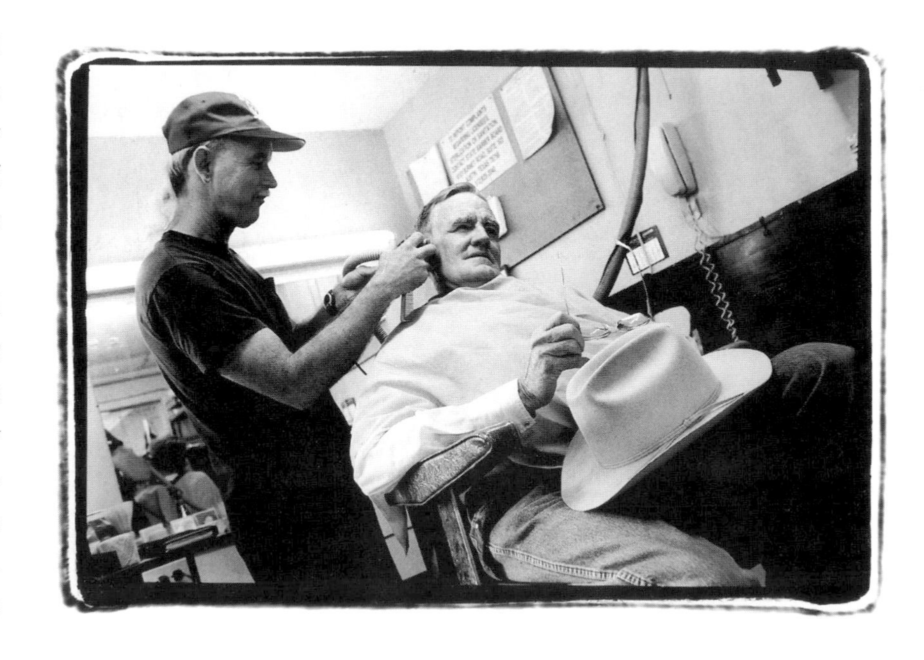

He and his wife do part-time sports officiating at youth baseball games, and he'd love to do that full time some day, he says.

In the meantime, the brother and sister remain in place at Brazos, where the gentle swish of the barber's clippers harmonizes with the buzz of the upright hairdryers. And the customers couldn't be happier—with their hair, or with themselves.

"You know what?" asks Pig Williams, not waiting for an answer. "If the man upstairs pulls the string on me tonight, well, I've had myself a ball." ■

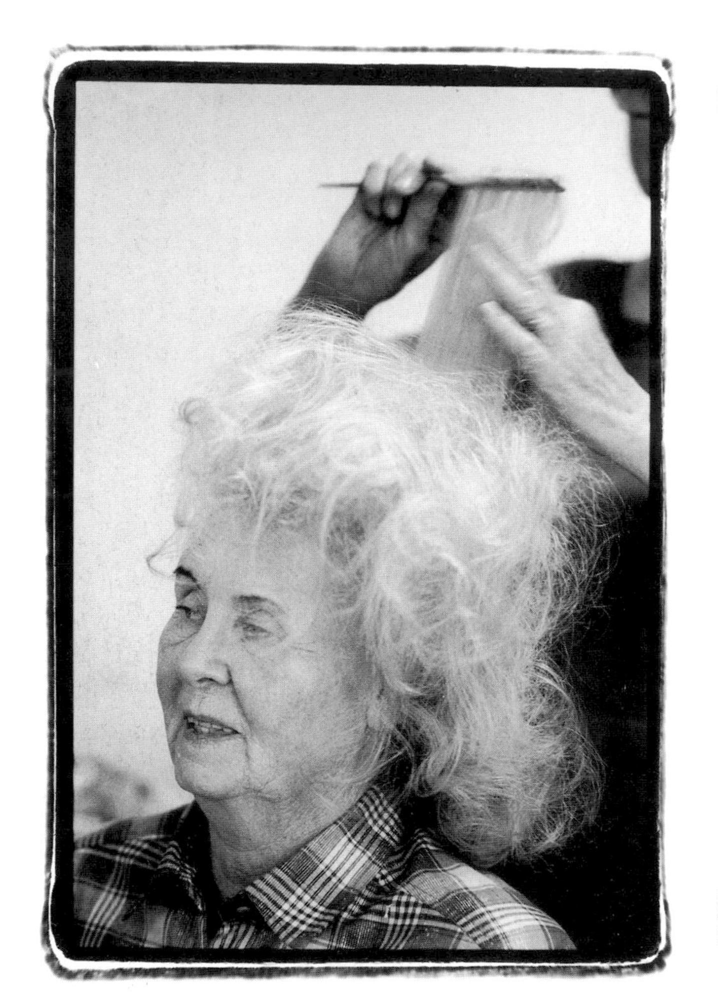

It only makes good sense that the nation's biggest state should produce some of the nation's biggest hair. In Texas, where the land stretches out in every direction, so do the best hairdos. Although not technically a Deep South state, Texas has produced a long line of Steel Magnolias, from the singing Mandrell Sisters to ascerbic ex-governor Ann Richards. Yippee-aye-oh, y'all.

Bobbie's Salon

DALLAS
TEXAS

In Bobbie's Salon a customer is poked and prodded and pulled into beautiful submission.

Carmen's Beauty Shop

FORT WORTH TEXAS

With customers falling asleep under the dryer, or giggling while getting a permanent, it's a wonder a few accidental deaths haven't rocked the beauty parlor industry. But in most shops, including Carmen's, the operators are highly trained in how to deal with potential disaster.

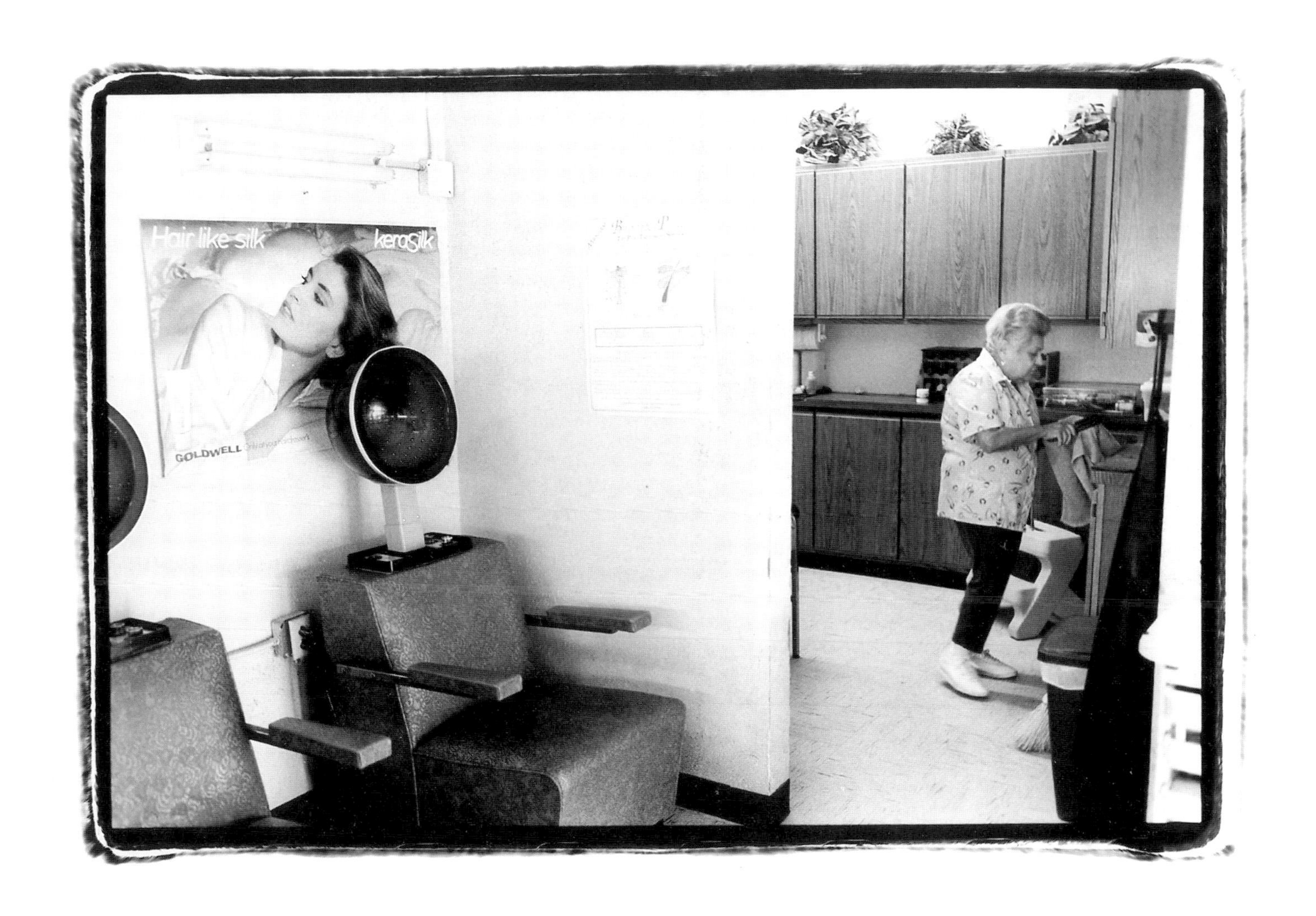

Owner Carmen Cisneros has presided over Carmen's for more than four decades. Like her equipment, she's getting on in years but is still in fine working order.

Hair Shack

PLANO
TEXAS

At Hair Shack a beautician practices what her little sign preaches. Along Main Street, the beauty parlor has thrived, while most other businesses have boarded up or moved away.

A beauty parlor can't have too many mirrors or hair dryers or pretty potions.

At Hair Shack customers are greeted and bid farewell with hugs.

About the Authors

Kathy Kemp

A native of Birmingham, Alabama, Kathy Kemp was a reporter at the *New Haven Register* in Connecticut before beginning a sixteen-year career as a feature writer and columnist with the *Birmingham Post-Herald.* Kathy recently joined the reporting staff of *The Birmingham News.*

Kathy is a two-time winner of the ASCAP/Deems Taylor Award for her stories about music. She won the Alabama Associated Press Sweepstakes Award in 1989 for her series on the Ku Klux Klan, and in 1994 she was runner-up for the Ernie Pyle Award. In 1996 Kathy was inducted into the Scripps Howard Newspapers Editorial Hall of Fame. She has been a regular contributor to *People* magazine and *The New York Times*.

With photographer Keith Boyer, Kathy has authored two other books, *Revelations: Alabama's Visionary Folk Artists* and *Welcome to Lickskillet and Other Crazy Places in the Deep South*.

Karim Shamsi-Basha

Born in Damascus in 1965, Karim Shamsi-Basha completed his undergraduate degree in mechanical engineering at the University of Tennessee. During his college years, Karim realized that his interest in photography was growing from hobby to love. He earned recognition for the depth of his photographs as well as for his ability to capture the emotion of any subject on black-and-white film.

In early 1990 Karim moved to Birmingham, Alabama, and joined the *Birmingham Post-Herald* staff. A self-taught photographer who learned primarily by trial and error, Karim has won many local, regional, and national awards, including Second Place for a sports photograph in the prestigious "Pictures of the Year" contest. He is an active member of the National Press Photographers Association.

In 1995 Karim opened his own photography studio and now completes assignments for *Time, Life, Newsweek, Sports Illustrated, Attaché, Coastal Living,* and other editorial clients. His photographs have appeared in major newspapers and magazines around the world.

Karim lives each day by the motto "Carpe diem" (Seize the day). He currently resides in Birmingham with his wife of thirteen years, Dee Tipps Shamsi-Basha, and their boys, two of the cutest children in the world. Six-year-old Zade, who received a camera on his first birthday, assists his dad and is an acclaimed photographer in his own mind. Two-year-old Dury finds empty film canisters irresistible and may also be an aspiring photographer.

Epilogue

"Honey, you just leave that bag right here and go get you a bite to eat. It will be right here when you get back . . . don't worry." That was the solution to lugging around my heavy camera bag at lunchtime when I was shooting photographs in a beauty shop in Texas.

In North Carolina I traded recipes with one of the wash-and-set regulars.

In Tennessee I made friends who I still keep in touch with from time to time.

In Georgia they called me "cream."

In Mississippi they trimmed my hair.

In South Carolina one shop just would not "buy" what I was "selling" (I still haven't figured out what I was selling).

In Alabama I helped fix a prehistoric hair dryer (I knew my mechanical engineering degree would come in handy someday).

In Louisiana I learned some French.

And in Florida I got another hair trim (actually it was a burr cut).

Traveling through nine Southern states and photographing beauty operators and their clientele is a once-in-a-lifetime experience that I may never top. As a freelance photographer I have covered everything from politicians to celebrities to athletes, but I have never met anyone whose life takes on a whole new look once a week as it does for these women. They get together at the same time and day every week in the same place and with the same people, but they always have a new experience. No one can explain it—the weekly beauty parlor appointment is a unique social phenomenon.

I wish someone had been videotaping when I walked into some of these shops unannounced. From under hair dryers and behind *National Enquirers,* pairs of grandmotherly eyes would follow me until I introduced myself to the owner and was greeted as a friend.

Then the ladies would say, "Oh . . . there's no way you are going to take my picture before my hair is finished." Or "Can you wait until I'm out from under the dryer?" Or "Wait until she wakes up!" As you can see from the uncensored photographs in this book, I didn't always do what they asked.

Karin Strauss-Baker

Birmingham, Alabama
August 1998